This first edition published in Great Britain and USA 2016
by Gene Keys Publishing
Suite 8864, 6 Slington House
Rankine Road Basingstoke RG24 8PH

Cover Design by Elijah Parker
& Teresa Collins

Richard Rudd
THE SEVEN SACRED SEALS
Portals To Grace

ISBN: 978-0-9569750-7-2

www.genekeys.com

CONTENTS

*The teachings in this book are
a passage into the invisible world that
lies beyond our ordinary senses.*

*To enter here is to court
the higher harmonies present
within the frequencies
of the inner Light.*

*May you feel the touch of
such energies in your life
and May Grace stroke your
soft head in her infinite tenderness.*

This book is dedicated to Beinsa Douno
(Peter Deunov of Bulgaria)

a man who knew and shared the inner light
at the deepest level.

THE SEVEN SACRED SEALS

PART 1
AN INTRODUCTION TO
THE SEVEN SACRED SEALS

THE CORPUS CHRISTI TEACHINGS

The Gene Keys transmission is a path of wisdom. It is a path that each person must walk in his or her own way, following the loopings and curvings of the pilgrim's way through a great and ancient body of world teachings that is vast in scope and rich in Truth. At the mystical heart of the Gene Keys is a set of teachings that form the basis of a new Mystery School. Known as the Corpus Christi, these teachings ripple out into the living matrix of the Gene Keys, bringing into form a sacred knowledge drawn directly from the higher realms.

If you are working with the Gene Keys in your life, whether you are reading the book or traveling one of the sequences of the Golden Path, the Corpus Christi delivers a powerful embodied context to the particular path you are taking. As I myself travel through these teachings, listening to and learning from the Gene Keys transmission, every now and then a special Ray falls to earth, and the Corpus Christi announces the time for a new revelation.

The Seven Sacred Seals are such a revelation. In fact they are more than an event, they are an initiation, in the deepest sense of the word. That they are coming into the world at this time is to me a miraculous occurrence because I sense that once they are at work in the world, a huge change will begin to take place. One might also look at this the other way around, that the Seals are coming because we are finally ready for them and because we have earned them.

As they come into the world, the Corpus Christi teachings lay out the canvas of a higher universal Truth. They provide us with nothing less than the living template of the true human, Homo Sanctus. Homo Sanctus refers to your future body, a Body of Light, sometimes also known as the Body of Glory or the Rainbow Body. Even though this body appears to have its full manifestation in the future, it exists inside us as a seed, alive in every moment, and at differing stages of evolution within each of us. The Corpus Christi describes and activates each of the seven layers of the Rainbow Body, through a series of transmissions, invocations and initiations. Some of these may occur as formal and collective events but most of the time these teachings are internal, occurring within our everyday lives.

THE SEVEN SACRED SEALS
A Revelation of St. John the Divine

The first recorded transmission of the Seven Sacred Seals was given in the Book of Revelations by St. John the Divine. This extraordinary testament is one of the great enduring mysteries of esoteric writing. It contains in coded form the living transmission of the Great Change — that epoch in which humanity will move through a complete transmutation before ascending to its final flowering. Having ascended to the highest peak of consciousness in the Ninth Initiation (see Gene Key 22), the spirit of Christ flooded the subtle bodies of his closest disciples, allowing them to access very high states of siddhic consciousness. This is what happened to John on his island retreat of Patmos, although it took some years to mature inside him.

Of all Jesus's disciples John stands alone as one gifted with great esoteric knowledge. The resurrection of his master propelled John to be the receiver of a transmission that very few have been gifted, or been able to survive. When we read the Revelation of St. John now it seems full of obscure imagery, metaphor and obtuse terminology. However, the truth of St. John's vision is far beyond human words to describe, which is why we can only penetrate this teaching if we can rise to a higher frequency ourselves. This is an ancient tradition in esoteric lore — that the highest teachings are written in a code woven from image and light that remains inaccessible to the lower frequencies of the human mind.

At the core of St. John's Revelation lies the teaching of the Seven Sacred Seals. Below is the definition from the Gene Keys Glossary of Empowerment:

The Seven Sacred Seals — The Seven Seals describe the specific pattern of awakening for humanity as the higher currents of involution and grace move over time through our species. Outlined in allegorical form in the Revelation of St. John, the unfolding of the Seven Seals can be understood as a sequential predestined awakening code hardwired into all human DNA. As each of the Seven Seals is mystically 'opened,' all aspects of the human wound, both individual and collective, will one day be healed. The teachings of the Seven Seals are contained within the transmission of the 22nd Gene Key, whose highest aspect is Grace. In the teaching of the Venus Sequence, you learn the precise science and underlying patterning of your suffering. As your awareness moves deeper into these Shadow patterns, you may become aware of the functioning of the Seven Seals as they affect your own individual awakening. At even deeper levels, you may become aware of how the Seven Seals are gradually opening up within the body of humanity. Such insights will lead to a great welling up of compassion and peace inside you.

So the key factor to understand the teaching of the Seven Sacred Seals is that they are a very refined frequency transmission that can only be activated and understood after considerable inner purification.

THE RING OF PURIFICATION
The Sublimation of Discord and Desire

If you wish to work with the Seven Sacred Seals in your life, you will need a fierce inner commitment. It may take many months of inner preparation before you receive signs that you are making progress. However, if your yearning is deep and sincere, a sustained effort will inevitably lead to a breakthrough. In the Gene Keys teachings, the secret of inner purification is guarded in the Codon Rings, and in particular by the Ring of Purification, which is a genetic grouping in human DNA that links together the 13th Gene Key and the 30th Gene Key.

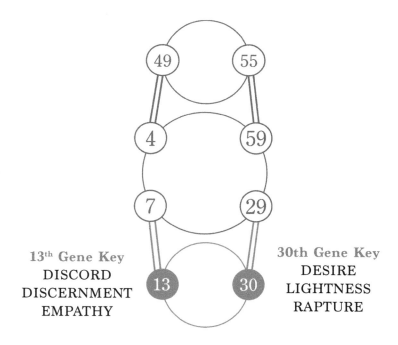

13th Gene Key
DISCORD
DISCERNMENT
EMPATHY

30th Gene Key
DESIRE
LIGHTNESS
RAPTURE

When you look at the Shadows of these two Gene Keys you will see the key to any serious course of purification. When we talk here of purification we are really talking about bringing about an upsurge in awareness around those patterns inside us that keep us at a low frequency.

PURIFICATION THROUGH THE 13TH GENE KEY

When you begin to work with the 13th Gene Key (it doesn't matter if you have it in your Profile or not), you will become much more adept at seeing through your negative patterns in your relationships. The 13th Gene Key teaches the art of inner listening. You listen to your own emotions and thought patterns and you listen to the way you react or respond both consciously and unconsciously when faced with confrontation. The Shadow of Discord is the inability to discern your own issues from the issues of others. This is why the Gift of Discernment opens inside you as you begin to pull out the emotional and mental weeds from the garden of your relationships.

This kind of purification is tough, backbreaking work! The only rewards come initially from your own quiet sense of victory as you manage to disable your Shadow patterns. An example might be not being pulled down into the lower frequencies of your own mind by the way someone else thinks about you or treats you. Relationships are all based on projection. We have to learn to purify our projections so that we only see the best in others, and at the same time, we must be consistently vigilant when it comes to our own Shadow projections. At a certain level of frequency, a beautiful disentanglement occurs in your key relationships. You are no longer pulled down into someone else's projection field but can retain your own high frequency no matter what the circumstances. This is the beginning of the Siddhi of Empathy.

PURIFICATION THROUGH THE 30TH GENE KEY

Working with the 30th Gene Key is a very private and internal process. It is the basis of all teachings that come under the label of 'Tantra.' Tantra refers to the gradual sublimation of our desire nature, and this 30th Gene Key has at its lower frequency the Shadow of Desire. It is important here to state that there is nothing wrong with any of the Shadow frequencies. They are the touchstones of the higher states. However, if you do not feel ready to sacrifice your lower desires to a higher goal, then this teaching is not suited to you at this time.

Working with the Shadow of Desire will take you into some challenging zones of consciousness. Our desire naturally shifts according to the seasons of our lives. Thus you will need to examine your daily urges and needs in depth and without any self-judgement. The important thing is just to see what forces are driving you, and how those forces tend to lead to further cycles of hunger and desire. The Gift of Lightness occurs as you begin to see how deeply you have allowed yourself to become a victim of your desires. Lightness here refers to two new qualities — the first is that as you begin to loosen the hold of your desires, you feel less heavy, both emotionally and mentally. You feel more buoyant and joyful. The patterns begin to let go on their own, just from your seeing them over and over again. In the early stages it is painful, but after some time, it almost becomes amusing to watch the soap opera of your desires playing out in your life.

The second quality that comes with the Gift of Lightness is literally that of light. You begin to feel incandescent, as though lit from within. This is because every desire you have can really be reduced to a single overarching desire — the desire to know your true nature. When you can trace this huge insight in your life, all your desires begin to serve the one goal — to purify your inner nature in order to experience the higher frequencies of your greater Self.

OPENING THE SEVEN SEALS USING THE VENUS SEQUENCE

As you begin to purify your inner being (a process which also happens naturally as you engage with the Gene Keys and the Golden Path), so you may one day be fortunate enough to experience the transmission of the Sacred Seals opening inside you.

Each of the Seven Seals is a very high frequency essence that is gifted to you at certain times in your life. As you work more deeply with the Gene Keys and particularly with your Venus Sequence, you will transmute the karma that you have generated over the course of your life. This karma often comes in the form of cellular memory from your childhood — for example — those deep patterns that occurred at crisis points in our early life, when we unconsciously closed off our heart and lost our natural sense of trust in life. Such memories have to be deeply felt and wrapped in our new awareness. This is not a comfortable experience as we are required to feel very vulnerable for periods of time, even as we go about our daily life.

THE VENUS SEQUENCE

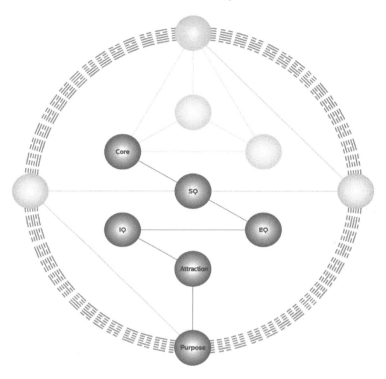

As your awareness tracks through your Venus Sequence, you will begin to see how the sequence naturally unlocks the old patterns inside you. This is an interactive transmission, brought alive through your relationships and the mirroring patterns that they provide. At points within the process, and usually after some considerable time, you will suddenly experience a breakthrough. Such an event, whether mental, emotional, physical, or all three, always results from the opening of one of the Seven Sacred Seals. It is as though the heavens open for a brief moment and the light pours through, opening you to a great inner vision of your higher self.

The teaching of the Seven Sacred Seals is directly analogous to the Venus Sequence. The Venus Sequence shows us the evolutionary path, as we strive to purify our hearts and minds in order to raise our frequency and re-set the original openness of our being. The Seven Seals on the other hand, show us the involutionary path, as the aspects of our higher self rain down upon us in infinite compassion, opening the gates of grace so that we can rethread the weave of our highest expression and purpose in the world.

GRACE AND THE SEVEN SIDDHIS

The Seven Sacred Seals and their respective Siddhis, lines and planes:

SEAL	SIDDHI	QUALITY	HEALS	BODY
The First Seal	40th	Divine Will	1st Line	Physical
The Second Seal	17th	Omniscience	2nd Line	Astral
The Third Seal	25th	Universal Love	3rd Line	Mental
The Fourth Seal	43rd	Epiphany	4th Line	Causal
The Fifth Seal	4th	Forgiveness	5th Line	Buddhic
The Sixth Seal	63rd	Truth	6th Line	Atmic
The Seventh Seal	22nd	Grace	All Lines	Monadic

If you are working with your Venus Sequence in depth you will soon realise that there is a certain configuration to the way your heart opens and closes. Each line number in your sequence is like the combination of a safe, and as you turn your awareness in these locks, they progressively open, along with your heart. Over time, the reward of the Venus Sequence is the permanent healing and opening of your heart. However, this rare occurrence can only come about through the activity of the Seven Seals.

In your healing process there will be moments of despair, moments of exultation and moments of pure Grace. Grace, the whole basis of these teachings, operates through each of the Seven Sacred Seals and their Siddhis. Each Siddhi is an outpouring of Divine energy or 'shakti' that works its way ever so subtly into our heart.

These six Siddhis of Grace each contain the specific antiserum that transmutes the six 'wounds' of the six lines. Therefore there is a deep mystery to these Siddhis of Grace. Each contains a specific transmission to heal an aspect of both the individual karmic wound and also the collective karmic wound of humanity. The Seventh Seal is the integrating field that brings the final culmination to this process of healing. For further insight on this you can read the 22nd Gene Key as well as the section on healing the Core Wound from Treading the Golden Path.

SERENDIPITY
A Side Effect of Grace

The transmission of the Seven Sacred Seals may at first appear complex to you or hard to comprehend but in truth it is simplicity itself. I recommend you thoroughly read and contemplate the 22nd Gene Key and work with the Venus Sequence (Part 2 of the Golden Path) in your relationships for a minimum of 9 months. After this period, the knowledge will have naturally found its way into you, and what once seemed complex to your mind will appear obvious. The Gene Keys wisdom and the Corpus Christi teachings are holographic in nature.

This means that as you imbibe their truths, they begin to create clarity at all seven levels of your being. However, this process takes time, courage and commitment.

One of the beautiful signs that this wisdom is opening inside you is the increased presence of serendipity in your life. Serendipity is a side effect of Grace. You will find that things in your outer life seem to flow more smoothly, and at the same time your inner world becomes more peaceful. Your physical body will learn to relax all on its own as you embrace the joy that comes from this increase in serendipity. Serendipity brings good fortune to you, it brings health and joyousness and a vision of a new possibility for a new kind of life. Embrace this wonderful gift of serendipity in your life. You are beginning to move in rhythm and harmony with a new higher kind of life. You are touching into the greater reality that is you. One day such a gift will lead you all the way to the Godhead itself, and then like St. John the Divine, you may even see the true face of God.

THE SEVEN SACRED SEALS

PART 2

THE SEVEN RAYS
OF LUMINESCENCE

'A man must have spiritual vision in order to perceive and comprehend the spiritual light of illumination. Then a magnificent world will be opened to him, a world in which illumination reigns. This illumination is both intelligent and alive, and all the great mystics who kindle it within themselves are able to see a boundless world, pulsating with the softest, most delicate and beautiful colours which fill their souls with streams of life.'

Beinsa Douno

The Light of Illumination

In order to truly come to know what life is, you will have
to come to a profound understanding of Light. Light as we
understand it in the physical world is only the tip of the
iceberg of this great subject. There is outer light, which we can
measure as vibrations of photons that appear to travel at a very
high but limited speed. Then there is inner light, which cannot
be measured and is limitless. But what is this inner light?
The mystics, masters and saints have spoken of it for millennia.
Is it simply a metaphor for something that cannot be put into
words?

It is the light of Illumination – a state or stage of consciousness
in which one becomes aware of faculties beyond the outer five
senses.

One senses that one is surrounded by light, or that one is
penetrated by light, or that one is radiating light, but this
light cannot be seen by the outer eye. In fact, the inner light is
brightest when we close our eyes. And not everyone senses this
light. Some people have never felt it. Others feel it sometimes
but not at others. Illumination is a great mystery.

The other aspect to Illumination is that it equates to love.

It seems to be the effect of love, and thus light and love have
always been connected in our understanding and our inner life.
No one who has felt deep love can deny that it seems to stream
from our heart, reaching out into the space around us and
connecting us to the object of our love, no matter how far away
that may be. True illumination does not even require an object
but pours through the soul as a feeling of utter gratitude and
heavenly bliss.

How then can we enter this other world beyond our senses? How can we bring about a state of illumination? These are questions that concern the teachings of the Seven Sacred Seals. These are teachings whose only goal is to bring about a deeper understanding of this other, hidden world, this world of the inner light. Therefore, when you begin to work with the Seven Sacred Seals, you are embarking on a different kind of journey. It is not a journey where logic prevails. It is not a journey that you can measure, unless you are measuring the amount of love you are capable of bearing. The journey into the Seven Sacred Seals is a journey beyond the frontiers where most people spend their lives. It is a passage into the world of Illumination, into the fabric of light that stitches both time and space together, and that will lead us one day into immensity, into that limitless world that we call the Divine.

THE SEVEN ANGELIC RAYS

When we look at a rainbow, we see light in a new and extraordinary way — we see it as colour. Goethe said that 'colours are the deeds and sufferings of light,' and his poetic insight may well be profound. Given the right conditions, white light explodes into the colours of the spectrum. One might imagine looking at a rainbow from the point of view of an early hunter-gatherer. In nature, bright colours are relatively rare, except perhaps in the tropics, where the full spectrum flowers in the jungles and the oceans. So the rainbow or the aurora has always been a place where a miracle resides. It opens us to the full spectrum of the possibilities that are pregnant in light.

Nowadays of course, colour is generally taken for granted. We have become so skilled at manipulating our environment that we can create and bend light to our will. And colour has lost some of its magic as well, through our scientific understanding, which reduces light to a series of frequencies, vibrations and wavelengths. But the visible spectrum and its seven primary colours has formed the foundation of a whole inner science based on the axiom of 'as above, so below.' Thus in many cultures we find that the number seven has taken on a special spiritual significance, and is the root of many mystical approaches to understanding the 'deeds and sufferings of light.'

In addition, because of its connection to the musical octave, the number seven bridges the two realms of sound and vision, and as a harmonic principle it connects us to the higher realms of the inner world. Seven is an angelic number, even forming the shape of the lyre or harp, which is the great symbol of the higher evolutions. Esoterically, all sacred teachings that centre on the number are gifts from these higher spheres of consciousness. In nature, each level of hierarchy is unable to comprehend the intelligence of the form that supersedes it. Thus most humans are not even aware of the evolutions that lie beyond us. The intelligence of what we call 'Angels' operates through the subtle bodies beyond the five senses. They are layers of consciousness that are far more organized and complex than our own. Therefore until we develop the higher faculties latent inside us, we cannot come into communion with such beings.

On the inner planes, the Seven Rays underpin the entire structure of the vibratory universe. Divine Light organizes consciousness through these seven fields and they can be unlocked through the transmission of the Seven Sacred Seals. When you begin to work with the Seals themselves, you will be directly invoking these seven Angelic frequencies.

PREPARING TO PERCEIVE THE INNER LIGHT

To perceive the inner light of illumination you must first move through the imagination. The creative imagination is the means by which inner light is given shape in the mind and heart. Such a realm exists at a higher frequency than our ordinary thinking mind, so you will not be able to enter it through visualization alone. The creative imagination must also be animated by a higher impulse, a spiritual longing that comes from your heart. This combination of aspiration and inspiration engages the causal body, our higher capacity to see the inner light. When you are able to contact your causal body, you will find yourself lifted into a higher dimension.

There are many ways to attain the use of your causal body — meditation, contemplation, prayer and other spiritual practice may all engage it. However, in order to inhabit your causal body with consistency, you must purify your life. Such purification involves considerable inner work.

You need a healthy diet and body. You need to refine your thoughts and weed out negative or self-limiting thought patterns. You also need to create a peaceful inner emotional environment, again weeding out self-destructive emotional patterns. Above all, you must lead a relatively peaceful and contemplative life. How else will you be able to perceive this inner light whose very basis is quietness and serenity?

Perhaps you can see that the path of opening the Seven Sacred Seals requires considerable inner discipline. It presupposes that you have already prepared the inner soil for such a quickening of consciousness. The good news is that most of these conditions are internal conditions that you can bring to fruition in your everyday life with some small adjustments. So the advice for anyone who wishes to work with the Seven Sacred

Seals is to do some inner spring cleaning before you begin. Take a good look at your life and simplify anything that adds more stress. Before you sow new seeds you must prepare the soil. You must clear away the weeds and add a rich fertilizer. The richer the soil, the more abundant your inner garden will become.

Working with the Gene Keys and in particular working with your Golden Path will help you greatly in respect to the above. The Golden Path is designed to pull out each weed — emotional, mental and physical, that prevents you from living a peaceful and contemplative life. Even in the fast-paced modern world, there is every opportunity for adapting your life to suit such a path. You may need to think and act creatively in order to bring it about, but once again, your Golden Path and the Gene Keys that lie threaded along it will guide you in this preparation to receive the inner Light.

THE SACRED SEALS ANGELIC MANDALA

USING THE ANGELIC MANDALA

The Sacred Seals Angelic Mandala acts as a visual foundation for the Seven Sacred Seals. This special mandala lays out the Seven Seals and their correspondences and sigils. A sigil acts as a magical talisman that has great power on the inner planes. This mandala is a symbolic conduit that draws upon the forces of Light and orchestrates them in your inner life. You can use the mandala for contemplation and also for protection. Because this teaching is rooted in the power of Grace, the mandala is an emanation of good fortune. It can be used as a talisman for counteracting negative forces in your inner life, and also in your outer life. By placing the mandala around your house or on your property you can use it to transmute negative karmic energies.

The creation of the Sacred Seals Angelic Mandala emerged through the same stream as the entire Gene Keys transmission and is therefore in direct resonance with this work. The names of the seven Archangels and their sigils are drawn from the Corpus Hermeticum — that ancient body of teachings that has passed through many cultures and epochs. In each of the seven sections of the mandala you will also see the corresponding name of a star and the quality that represents the action of the inner light connected with that star and its Seal. As you move towards the centre of the mandala you will see the Siddhi or Divine attribute that is behind the Seal itself. Moving further inwards we come to the essence of the inner light on the angelic spectrum, and finally we can see its associated Gene Key and hexagram in the I Ching.

As you begin to work with the Seven Sacred Seals you will become deeply acquainted with this magical mandala and you will learn to unlock its many layers of meaning and use. First and foremost it is designed to be used as a contemplative tool to invoke the higher frequencies of these seven great Siddhis of Grace, Truth, Forgiveness, Epiphany, Love, Omniscience and Divine Will.

It can also be used inwardly in times of distress or challenge, and just by gazing at it, you can let its higher meanings pervade your consciousness, bringing you much solace during times of conflict.

The Seven Rays in the Angelic Spectrum

When we convert the seven colours of our earthly spectrum into their higher counterparts on the higher planes of consciousness, we enter the hallowed world of the Angelic Spectrum — a kaleidoscopic array of inner light that cannot be perceived by ordinary human senses. Light within the Angelic Spectrum cannot easily be categorized or described in human language.

The closest we can come is by using the creative imagination to invoke the feeling behind the light. You have to enter this inner world with such delicacy and subtlety, and when you are able to open yourself to these higher frequencies you will perhaps be graced to feel the swirling currents and emanations of the pure light as it flickers through your aura. Below are brief mythical descriptions of the Seven Rays that can be opened by the Seven Sacred Seals:

Ray 1 - Incandescence
The 40th Siddhi - Divine Will - Archangel Mikael

Incandescence is a white/gold emanation that mythically flares around the sword of Archangel Mikael. The role of this inner light is to grub out the deepest roots of our ancestral karma. This is the inner light of Deliverance, which provokes, challenges and transmutes the dragon within our DNA. This is a vanquishing light, although it does not conquer through force but by the intensity of its love. The quality of Incandescence is like a lonely candle flame burning in the window of a faraway home within the depths of an icy, dark winter landscape. Like a warm hearth, it calls you home from your many exhausting travels and trials. This imagery conjures up something of the texture of Incandescence.

RAY 2 - PHOSPHORESCENCE

The 17th Siddhi - Omniscience - Archangel Khamael

Phosphorescence is a sharp crystal blue emanation that burns like the Eye of God. The archangel Khamael, whose name means 'he who sees God,' represents the force that brings an end to suffering through absolute vision. This inner light glows softly but with infinite precision to allow the receiver to see the perfection of their presence within the universal story. Humans know phosphorescence through the tiny lights emitted by bacteria and plankton living in the sea at night. This is the gentle aspect of this inner light. However, the other side is caught by the incredibly bright white blueish light that one sees when phosphorus burns. Phosphorescence actually emerges from within human DNA, which is made up of phosphates.

RAY 3 - RUBESCENCE

The 25th Siddhi - Universal Love - Archangel Raphael

Rubescence is a wonderful quality of red/gold light that equates to the Siddhi of Universal Love. Everything that is alive hums with this radiant, warming light. Rubescence can be fanned and increased within the human organism by the presence of love. It is the afterglow of love and is deified in the image of Archangel Raphael, whose name means 'he who heals.' Indeed this light is deeply soothing in the organism and can bring about miraculous healing through DNA repair.

This inner light is also associated with the final goal of alchemy — the 'rubedo' — the dawn of the crimson/gold light of the philosopher's stone — the full awakening of human beings into their inner royalty.

RAY 4 - IRIDESCENCE
The 43rd Siddhi - Epiphany - Archangel Haniel

Iridescence is a rainbow emanation that awakens, vivifies
and catalyzes breakthroughs on the inner planes. It is like
a sudden visitation from a bright iridescent dragonfly. It
has an almost electrical charge that constantly flickers and
changes colour, engendering a sense of playfulness and awe.
The quality of iridescence is linked to the Archangel Haniel,
whose name means 'Joy of God.' This is the light of epiphanies
— breakthroughs from the higher planes accompanied by a
swelling of joyousness and naturally occurring ecstatic states.
Iridescence is also an inner light associated with children and
the honouring of the Divine Inner Child symbolized by the
Christian Epiphany.

RAY 5 - PEARLESCENCE
The 4th Siddhi - Forgiveness - Archangel Tsadkiel

Pearlescence is a soft, subtle silver/grey emanation that instead
of radiating light, softens and diffuses all energy that it comes
in touch with. Pearlescence has a deeply feminine quality
connected to the underwater world of pearls and mother-of-
pearl. You can also imagine the sounds of such an environment
being connected to the quality of silence in this Ray.
Pearlescence is the light of the Siddhi of Forgiveness, which is
deified in the figure of the Archangel Tsadkiel, traditionally a
Divine symbol of the quality of mercy and forgiveness. A vast
emanation, pearlescence is a key aspect of Divine Grace as it
moves down into the world of form.

RAY 6 - QUIESCENCE

The 63rd Siddhi - Truth - Archangel Gabriel

Quiescence is an emanation whose essence is beyond the colours of words. You might call it colourless, but it has more to do with silence. It is the colour of silence and its presence will stop all thoughts. Think of a cold clear winter's night with the snow falling or the silence of an owl's flight, and you may begin to have a sense of the magic of quiescence. Quiescence is also the emanation of Truth, the 63rd Siddhi, which is traditionally known in the I Ching as 'After Completion.' Quiescence is about the utter rest and completion that comes after the revelation of Truth. This is the emanation of Gabriel, the Archangel who it is said will blow the final trumpet on the Day of Judgement.

RAY 7 - LUMINESCENCE

The 22nd Siddhi - Grace - Archangel Tsaphkiel

Luminescence is akin to the white light of the outer senses that contains each of the hidden layers of the rainbow spectrum. Luminescence contains and gathers up all the other Rays. Each Ray is an emanation of Divine Grace, that wordless quality that passes human understanding but that periodically visits the physical plane. The quality of luminescence is a royal cobalt blue emanation fringed with gold, like the dusk sky on a perfect spring night. The air is alive with the bursting energy of growth and possibility, and the mystery of the first dawning stars stroke the earth with their spectral light. In the Kabbalah, the Archangel Tsaphkiel rules over the sphere of Binah, the Divine Feminine. Grace is a feminine emanation that falls from heaven to earth, and luminescence is the texture of that ineffable light.

OPENING THE SEVEN SACRED SEALS

Each of the Seven Rays of the subtle realms is hidden behind a seal — a kind of Divine valve that can only be opened when there is resonance between that which is below and that which is above. This is why we have to go through periods of purification — to raise our frequency to such a pitch that it triggers the valve to open and the light to descend. The Seven Sacred Seals is therefore a transmission that requires inner work and courage. It is a calling out for Grace and therefore involves invocations, prayers and formulas that accompany and strengthen our contemplation.

It is important to realise that the Seven Rays of the Angelic Spectrum are far more than simply rays of light. They are fields of living intelligence — aspects of our higher consciousness. They are the vestments of the beings that we call the Archangels. Thus if you receive the grace of a visitation from one or more of these planes through the opening of one or another of the Seven Seals, it will be far more than an experience within your imagination. It will have a profound impact on your whole inner being. A door will open on a world that you have probably never touched into since you were a very young child. And all manner of blessings can emerge through this door into your life.

When you are in the presence of a very young child, you may be able to detect the subtle aura of the light that surrounds them. Sometimes you will have the impression that they are looking at things in the surrounding space that you cannot see. The infant in their first few years of life swims in this inner world of light. They come to the earth plane trailing the other world with them, and the beings from this other world are attracted to their purity and their untarnished innocence.

It is every adult's highest potential to regain this state of illumination, but to do so they must move through a profound healing of their deepest Core Wound — the ancestral genetic pattern that they also brought with them when they incarnated.

THE SEVEN SACRED SEALS

PART 3

OPENING THE SEALS, INVOKING GRACE
& HEALING THE CORE WOUND

THE SEVEN SEALS AS A HIGHER TANTRA

The Gene Keys transmission is in essence a tantric teaching.
Tantra, in the form of inner alchemy, is a process of gradual
sublimation of base karmic residue into more refined spiritual
essence. Our particular spiritual path in life unwinds according
to the dictates of the karma we have accumulated both in this
life and our past incarnations. Most authentic tantric traditions,
such as the Buddhist Vajrayana, divide the tantric teachings into
broad levels. The 'Root Tantra' forms the basis of the higher
practices and is more widely accessible, whereas the higher
practices are usually more secret and are generally transmitted
orally by a Master.

In the case of the Gene Keys Transmission, you could say that
the Root Tantra is the Golden Path. It gives you the basis
of the spiritual labour you are here to undertake. The most
profound work within the Golden Path is the Venus Sequence,
which shows us how to release and transmute the many karmic
patterns that keep us from experiencing the pure love of our
untarnished heart.

For most people, this work with the Golden Path is enough for
their whole lifetime. However for some, their karmic disposition
will lead them further and deeper inwards. Once the heart
begins to heal and open on a more permanent basis, then
another higher level beckons us. This is called the Diamond
Path. The Diamond Path is represented by the single Pathway
that leads from the Sphere of your SQ (Spiritual Quotient) to
the Sphere of the Core Wound.

The journey along the Diamond Path is a journey you must take
alone. It is an intense inner calling in which the light from your
Core beckons you progressively to enter into the silent layers of
the inner luminescence. It is the Path of Spiritual Absorption.

THE DIAMOND PATH

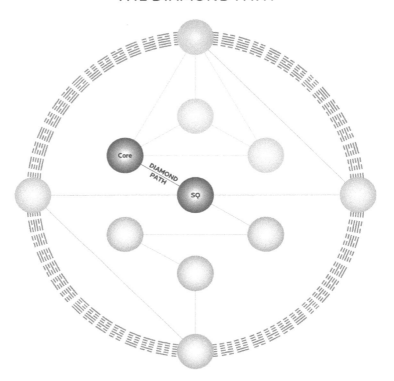

Within this framework, the Seven Sacred Seals have two applications. The first is as an initiation for anyone, through the medium of the Seventh Seal. The Seventh Seal is the great Seal of Grace that will open to any who call upon it with a genuine, heartfelt voice. It is both the beginning and the end of the Path. Its secrets are open for all to partake, rooted as it is in the open generosity of the Divine Feminine principle. However, the second application of the Seven Seals concerns the higher form of Tantra known as the Completion Stage, which dawns as our heart opens and as we prepare to embark on the Diamond Path of Realization. This is a six-branched tantra intended for Initiates on the inner path.

THE SEVENTH SEAL

THE RING-PASS-NOT OF THE SEVENTH SEAL

In the mysterious coils of the Seven Seals teachings, the Seventh Seal also contains a hidden inner doorway. This is a mystical portal through which only those who are ready may pass. Such a doorway is known in the mysteries as a 'Ring-Pass-Not' because it can only be accessed by those who have the right code. In this case, the right code refers to an open or a readily 'opening' heart. This higher teaching embedded within the Seven Seals therefore remains dormant unless you are working intensely with the Golden Path or with other authentic materials or teachers that assist you in transmuting your inner karma.

The higher Seven Seals teachings include formulas, exercises and prayers that involve deeply subtle dimensions. It is therefore recommended that you use them alongside the Golden Path, and in particular the Venus Sequence, when you feel called to use them.

It is important to say that there is no danger whatsoever in performing any of these exercises associated with the Seven Seals or in the higher tantric teachings themselves. However, you will know when you are ready to employ the teachings of the Seals because you will feel an intuitive draw to them, and your heart will rise up inside them, which is what makes them so powerful.

The best advice for newcomers is to begin working exclusively with the Seventh Seal and its Invocation and the beautiful prayers in this book. After some time, you will experience the Grace of this Seal moving in your life, opening you in unexpected ways. Then, when you feel ready, you can ask inner permission of the teachings to work with the other six Seals. Your own self-honesty will be a deep part of your healing in this regard. Our spiritual ego may tend to want us to progress more rapidly than we actually can. This can be a deep lesson in humility and patience because if you embark on the higher path before you are genuinely ready, you will simply find the higher frequencies barred from your view and your practice may fall flat. If this occurs, it is a useful lesson and we can be grateful for it!

THE SQ AND THE OCEAN OF LOVE

In your Hologenetic Profile, at the heart of your Venus Sequence lies the Sphere of your SQ — your spiritual quotient. Your spiritual quotient is a measure of how much love you are able to bring into the world. However, when we speak of love here, we are not speaking of emotional love but the intelligence of unconditional love — a white hole within every human being through which great wisdom and truth can come into the world. Our SQ begins to contract during the first seven years of life as we gradually (or suddenly) come into contact with the frequency of fear embedded in humanity. Simply understood, the stronger your spiritual aspiration is, the more in touch you are with this love in your SQ.

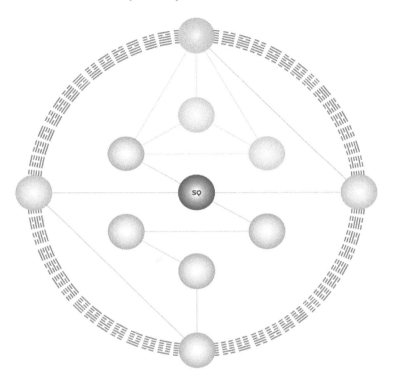

In the Venus Sequence, your awareness learns to travel back in time through the layers and memories of your wounding (your 'sanskaras') until it reaches right down into the depths of this great dammed-up ocean of love. As your awareness begins to penetrate your SQ and its cellular memory, cracks begin to appear in the walls that you learned to build around your heart as a child. When this happens, you will experience periodic rushes or waves of love. These breakthroughs intensify as your awareness continues to gather itself around the hurt in your heart. This is both an ongoing uncomfortable and sometimes agonizing experience as well as an exalting and ecstatic one and it requires a very soft touch and deep patience. This heart opening period may go on for a considerable time, probably even years.

THE FOURTH INITIATION OF MATRIMONY

The above experience of the gradual opening of the love inside our hearts represents a period of inner Initiation in our lives. All Initiation involves such a period of breakthroughs, and each Initiation is different in its scope and flavour. In the Corpus Christi teachings, there are a total of nine Initiations arranged in trinities. This breaking through of love within us relates to the Fourth Initiation, known as The Matrimony. The Fourth Initiation is the higher octave of the First Initiation of Birth, that extraordinary time in a person's incarnative story when they first become aware that they have an inner life, and they take the first tentative steps to explore that life. In this sense, the Fourth Initiation is another kind of Birth — a Rebirth, as we reclaim the inheritance of our childhood innocence and bring it alive once again within our adult life.

THE NINE INITIATIONS

9. Glorification
8. Sanctification
7. Ordination

6. Communion
5. Annunciation
4. Matrimony

3. Confirmation
2. Baptism
1. Birth

The Fourth Initiation of Matrimony culminates in a great flood of love as the dam finally bursts and we experience the permanent opening of our spiritual heart. This is the mystical sacred marriage spoken of by many esoteric traditions. We become married to love itself, and we know in every cell of our body that this is now a permanent state of Grace. Even death will not part us from this knowing, and our mystical union is a major milestone on our spiritual journey. Never again will we be caught in the trap of looking for love in the outer world. We enter a new world where our life is the groom and our love is the bride, and our eternal wedding is now signed and sealed for all to see.

We cannot know when such an Initiation will occur to us, but our life journey gives us some indication. The period leading to the Initiation is also a part of the Initiation, just as the engagement period before a marriage is also a part of the marriage. It is a period of intensity, of inner change, anticipation, challenge and letting go. It is during this extended period that the teaching of the Seven Sacred Seals can be a great help to us. It is designed for those who are doing the deep inner work of heart-opening, taking us all the way to the Fifth Initiation — the Annunciation, where the Diamond Path begins in earnest.

THE SIX-BRANCHED TANTRA OF THE COMPLETION STAGE

When you are ready to move deeper into the sacred wound inside, you can begin to work with all the Seven Sacred Seals. Once you have opened up the field of this wisdom with the Seventh Seal, you can move through each of the other 6 Seals in turn. These should be approached in a sequence beginning with the Sixth Seal and culminating with the First Seal. The reason for this reverse sequence is that we are bringing the higher consciousness progressively down through the layers of the subtle bodies as we open each Seal.

The First Seal therefore is about suffusing the physical body with this higher consciousness, having first brought it down through both the mental and emotional layers.

This process of working with the 6 Seals in progression has the purpose of purifying the karma you carry in your DNA. We each carry both personal karma from this life and our past incarnations as well as collective karma, which we carry on behalf of the whole. Although this karma is commingled inside us, generally speaking we have to purify our personal karma first before we can tackle the collective ancestral karma. We experience this karma as tightness, numbness, constriction and discomfort in our physical, emotional and mental bodies. During this advanced stage, it is assumed that your contemplative practice is already deep and consistent, so that you can bring your awareness and self-compassion to this discomfort with equanimity, rather than letting it make you over-anxious. If you do feel at any point that it is too much for you to bear, you should immediately cease the practice and return to the Seventh Seal and its Invocation and prayers, calling upon Grace to bring you back into balance.

Working with the 6 Seals, your contemplation will naturally deepen even more as you unlock older residues of karma within the sheaths of your subtle bodies. You should stay with each Seal long enough for it to bring you some kind of expansion (this may take a considerable time). There is no point in moving to the next Seal unless you have experienced the benefits of the present one, as once again you will find that your practice falls flat.

Eventually, your contemplative practice will take you through all of the 6 Seals until you arrive at the First Seal, which concerns the physical body itself.

By the time you have come this far, you will have experienced many phases and transitions in your inner journey. Revelations may come; insights may flicker in your mind as well as memories of a mental, emotional or cellular nature. Remember, the entire process is completely safe because your heart can only transmute the amount of karma equivalent to its state of openness.

Once you have completed the 6 branches of this phase of the Completion Practice, you can then begin to work more deeply with any specific Seal of your choice. When you look at your Venus Sequence you will find that the most powerful Seals for you tend to be the ones that relate to the line numbers of your SQ and your Core Wound. In other words, if you have a 6th line SQ, then you can work with the Sixth Seal, and if you have a 5th line Core Wound, then you can work with the Fifth Seal. There is no time limit to this inner work, although you will find that it greatly accelerates the process of inner alchemy and purification that you are doing at this stage.

TANTRA AND MAGICK, BUDDHA AND CHRIST
The Merging of East and West

The Seven Sacred Seals flow from the heart of the Gene Keys transmission, and this transmission of wisdom is rooted in Synthesis.

As such, the Seven Seals also carry this spirit of unifying esoteric Truth from the East and the West. From the Eastern perspective, we have already seen that the Seals themselves are a Tantric teaching. They flow from the tradition of Deity

Tantra, a process in which the Initiate creates inside him or herself a potent identification with a particular Deity, an internal manifestation of a Divine Ideal. Over time, the qualities and Siddhis of this Deity are transferred into the consciousness of the Initiate.

The great Tantric systems, although rooted in the earlier Vedic traditions, really came into their fullest manifestation after the birth of the Buddha. Out of the Buddha's realization sallied forth a whole stream of transmissions, some taught by him personally, others taught on the inner planes by his bodhisattvic emanations in the generations following his birth. A whole host of masters also appeared in his wake, carrying the 'Termas' (secret wisdom streams) into the various cultures that embraced the essence of this living wisdom. You can still find the vibrant heart of this Tantra in the various traditions where it spread to the East. You will find it in the Taoist, Zen, Tibetan and Buddhist schools, as well as in the Himalayan traditions such as Kriya Yoga and Raja Yoga. There are even echoes of it in the higher devotional teachings of Sufism. Transmissions are not limited by geography or time, but emanate wherever Divine Grace manifests as a being of great love and wisdom.

In the West, the same stream of esoteric alchemical lore flowed out of the living tradition of the Christ. Christ's love contains the same Truth as the Buddha's compassion, although in a slightly different style or 'Ray.' In the West, the same transmission is encoded in the Kabbala, which predates the historical Jesus but was greatly enriched through his manifestation as the Christ. This aspect of the ancient teachings continued to propagate through the secret lore of the alchemists and through the Hermetic teachings of high Magick. Just as the code was deified in the Eastern traditions, so too it was deified in the West through the figures of the angels and archangels, and through the further manifestations of Christ as the various saints.

It is important to allow this inner symbolism to find a way inside you when you come to the Seven Seals teachings.

You need to find your own inner correlations in the cultures and beings that you can relate to. If for example, you feel drawn to a particular Divine manifestation, then you need to draw yourself closer into that field. Ultimately, this teaching is about fully identifying yourself as that Divine manifestation. It invites you to cross the threshold of worship into full embodiment. However, once the embodiment has occurred, the manifestation reveals itself simply as a means to access the peerless state of Divine emptiness.

A UNIVERSAL PANTHEON
Tantric Deities and Saints

Below are the correlations of the seven great Tantric Bodhissatvas and Saints from the Buddhist and Christian traditions placed alongside the Seven Sacred Seals and their Archangels.

BODHISSATVAS	SAINTS	ARCHANGELS	SEALS
Tara	Mother Mary	Tsaphkiel	7th Seal
Maitreya	St. Thomas	Gabriel	6th Seal
Amitabha	St. Teresa	Tsadkiel	5th Seal
Padmasambhava	St. Paul	Haniel	4th Seal
Avalokitesvara	St. Francis	Raphael	3rd Seal
Manjushri	St. John	Khamael	2nd Seal
Kalachakra	St. Peter	Mikael	1st Seal

In both pantheons you can see that the Seventh Seal anchors the Feminine essence, which enfolds all other manifestations. In many cases these figures also had consorts or feminine poles, which can also be explored through contemplation. It is important to realise that these beings are really inner representations of Divine attributes and Siddhis, so although you may find historical references to them, it is their inner quality that is most important in this teaching. Having said that, such beings have independent existence on the Buddhic planes of reality. When Grace alights on you, then a spontaneous visitation from any higher being is possible and can have a hugely beneficial impact inside you.

THE SEVEN TANTRIC BODHISSATVAS

THE SEVENTH SEAL
Tara (Mother of Liberation)

Tara is the great Female Divinity of Tibetan Tantra. She is an egregor of a multitude of emanations of Divine Grace which are registered as a spectrum of colours — for example, White Tara represents compassion whereas Green Tara represents enlightened action.

THE SIXTH SEAL
Maitreya (Loving Kindness)

Maitreya is the long-prophesied future Buddha who is said will be the successor of Gautama, the historical Buddha. There are many legends around Maitreya, one of the most potent is that he may incarnate not as a single person but as a group soul, opening humanity's potential to embody the Truth at a collective level.

THE FIFTH SEAL
Amitabha (Infinite Light)

One of the oldest Bodhissatvas, Amitabha is a celestial Buddha of comprehensive love. Often connected to longevity, Amitabha is said to have created the Pure Land of the Buddhic Plane itself. His most potent meditation is to see the present world as a living paradise.

THE FOURTH SEAL
Padmasambhava (Lotus-born)

One of the most mysterious Bodhissatvas, Padmasambhava is the great revealer of Termas (hidden treasures or 'transmissions' of wisdom) that are to be opened at specific times in history. Padmasambhava is also strongly connected to the Tantric revelation known as the Rainbow Body.

THE THIRD SEAL
Avalokitesvara (Compassionate Lord of the World)

Possibly the most widespread Bodhissatva, Avalokitesvara absorbs within himself all ancient traditions and manifests through a vast array of otherworldly forms symbolized by his 1,000 arms. Both male and female in many of his manifestations, he is connected to the ideal of Universal Love and compassion.

THE SECOND SEAL
Manjushri (Transcendent Wisdom)

Manjushri is an ancient Bodhissatva known throughout the Orient and with particularly strong connections to China. Depicted with a flaming sword, he is known as a being whose great wisdom can cut through all attachments or confusion. His transmission flows through the Zen as well as the Taoist traditions.

THE FIRST SEAL
Kalachakra (Wheel of Time)

Kalachakra is both a deity and a set of complex higher Tantric practices for attaining enlightenment. The transmission of Kalachakra is generally known as the peak of all dharma. It is deeply connected to the mythical manifestation of Shambhala, the magical higher core of Gaia's consciousness.

THE SEVEN TANTRIC CHRISTIAN SAINTS

THE SEVENTH SEAL
Mother Mary

As the Mother of Christ and the Holy Madonna, Mary or
Marian has long been known as the great archetype of the
Divine Mother. Her presence on the inner planes brings
Divine Tenderness and Solace that surrounds and suffuses all
beings. Mary represents the Grace that can always be called
upon in any situation, particularly where there is suffering.

THE SIXTH SEAL
St. Thomas

Sometimes known as 'Doubting Thomas,' St. Thomas was
one of the 12 disciples of Jesus and carries a powerful 'tantric'
theme — that of overcoming doubt in order to attain Truth.
The Gospel of St. Thomas carries a very potent transmission of
the sayings of Jesus with all the narrative stripped out. Thomas
is also said to be the only disciple present at the Assumption of
Mary, as she ascended to heaven.

THE FIFTH SEAL
St. Teresa

Teresa of Avila was a medieval mystic who attained very
high states of ecstatic God-consciousness. She had a series of
embodied visions in which Christ became visible to her. These
experiences gave her a lifelong understanding of the nature of
sin and the means to transcend it through a kind of four-level
'Christian Tantra.'

THE FOURTH SEAL
St. Paul

St. Paul is another renowned Christian figure, best known
for his sudden conversion or Epiphany en route to Damascus,
when he was struck blind by an intense vision of the
resurrected Christ. After this, St. Paul became one of the
greatest apostles of Christ, and much of the New Testament is
attributed to him.

THE THIRD SEAL
St. Francis

One of the best known and most fondly-loved of all Christian
Saints, St. Francis represents the vast humility of the love
for all humans and creatures, no matter how insignificant
they may seem. St. Francis's life is also a representation of
the complete surrender of the lower self into the arms of the
Divine.

THE SECOND SEAL
St. John

One of the closest of Christ's disciples, John appears to
have the very special role and Gift of understanding and
communicating Divine Wisdom. St. John the Divine (as he is
also known) travelled to Patmos in Greece where he received
the Book of Revelation — the most arcane and hidden tantric
'terma' of the Christian pantheon.

THE FIRST SEAL
St. Peter

Jesus's first disciple, St. Peter represents the 'rock' upon which
the entire teaching of Christ is founded. Peter's faith is tested

by Jesus many times, and becomes steadily strengthened. His martyrdom on an inverted cross sings out with a great tantric symbolism that ultimately led to his being given the 'keys' to heaven.

The above Pantheon of Tantric Holy figures from both Buddhist and Christian traditions is included here as a source of deeper contemplation that can run beneath the Seven Sacred Seals.

The Seals are magical in origin and primarily invoke the power of the Seven Archangels and the Seven Stars in the heavens. However, the source of this transmission predates all historical and religious figures. This Pantheon is therefore included as a guideline for you to find your own intuitive connections to the many beings who populate the higher planes of reality.

GENE KEYS STAR LORE
Capturing the Firmament

An important aspect of the Seven Sacred Seals teaching is as a means of aligning the macrocosm to the microcosm. The seven stars are an ancient teaching connected to both the seven stars of the Great Bear and the Seven Sisters of the Pleiades. Each of the Seals is a portal to a field of higher consciousness and each of these fields has a connection to seven great portals to celestial Grace in the firmament. Every Gene Key has a relationship to a particular star and thus the seven stars that relate to the Seven Seals have a deep import on our place within the cosmos.

The stars in the night sky are far more than balls of helium and hydrogen — they are the physical manifestations of those inner plane entities that we call Angels and Archangels.

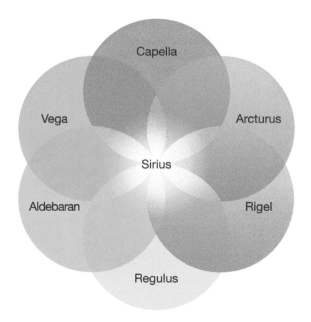

As you align your own energies to these star systems, whether through gazing up at them or through using creative imagination or both, you are effectively expanding your consciousness to encompass the macrocosm. The light from these seven stars may take trillions of years to reach us across outer space, but in the silent vacuum of inner space, their light is already here. Their frequencies glow inside our aura, and as we fan their radiance, so their qualities and intelligence come alive inside us. This is the basis of Alchemical Star Lore, an extraordinary tool that we humans will use in the future as a way of connecting into our greater body — the universe.

HEALING THE CORE WOUND
Preparations and Practices

By now you will have a fuller sense of the enormous depth of the teachings and transmission of the Seven Sacred Seals. These are tools that you can use over a long period of time, and as you use them, they will increase the frequency of light flashing through your aura.

Over time, they will illuminate your mind and open your heart. Their final role is to prepare us to make the transition from the Fifth Initiation of Annunciation to the Sixth Initiation of Communion. As mentioned earlier, this is known as the Diamond Pathway of Realisation. This inner Pathway will open as your awareness rethreads its path back through the nine months of gestation until it arrives at the point of your conception. Like the salmon, your awareness must return to its source, where you will finally surrender your separate identification with the form of your body. This is the stage of final enlightenment, which is also referred to as the 'healing of the sacred wound.'

THE CORE WOUND

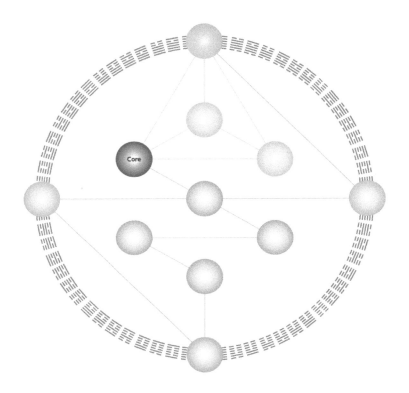

The Seven Sacred Seals prepare us to take this final journey, and they make use of many practices. Chief among these is your ongoing Contemplation of and identification with the Deities, Stars and Siddhis. In addition to this central technique, there are a host of other practices to support your Contemplative journey. These are listed below.

THE INVOCATIONS

The seven Invocations are very powerful inner callings that
we can resonate over and over again inside our being. We can
perform the invocations externally, through reading them
aloud in a ritualistic way, or we can do them internally.
The power of invocation is that it fuses the three lower bodies,
the physical, astral and mental, with the three higher bodies,
the causal, buddhic and atmic. You need therefore to be
physically, emotionally and mentally engaged as you perform
the Invocations. Over time, they will enter more deeply into
your inner consciousness where they will keep opening up the
Sacred Seals themselves.

THE PRAYERS

There are also specific prayers that go along with these teachings,
and these can be used at any time. Prayer is a means of creating
intimacy between you and your higher Self. Like Invocation, it is
an upward-moving force, but it is much more distilled. You can
also create your own prayers, either spontaneously or formally,
in order to translate your evolutionary impulse into a code that
is then transmitted into the higher dimensions of your Self.
The most important factor about Prayer is to ensure it is always
selfless and transparent, and that you let your heart rise up in
the prayer.

THE BLESSINGS

Like the Prayers, the Blessings can be used at any time.
However, a blessing has a different purpose from a prayer.
The blessing asks for a very specific kind of anointing. It invites
the Shakti of the higher planes to descend in the moment and

touch us with its Grace. Prayer does not ask for this direct response but is more open-ended. The Blessing is immediate, which means that you must prepare yourself beforehand and then bow your whole being in order to receive the Grace of the Blessing.

INCANTATIONS, CHANTS AND MANTRAS

In addition to the above practices, you can also add your own exercises in the form of songs or chants. Letting the music of your voice ring out with your own Holy intent is one of the most powerful and universal ways of expressing your higher yearning for sacred union. Many of the Deities mentioned above have specific mantras that can be used, although it is important to pronounce them correctly as each root syllable forms a part of the overall sonic signature. Singing in unison or harmony with others also enhances the process of all the above, and is highly recommended.

MUDRAS

Each of the Seven Sacred Seals has a 'mudra,' a specific hand position used in meditation to increase and harmonize with the frequency of the Siddhi of that Seal. These mudras are very powerful and should be used with care as they create hidden rhythms and ripples throughout our subtle bodies. These are in turn transmitted into our nervous system, which can be overloaded if we are not prepared and listening inwardly. The Mudra of the Seventh Seal is the safest and most universally beneficial to use, and you can always adopt it to bring your system back into balance.

YANTRAS AND MANDALAS

For those with a strong visual bent, the creation of personal mandalas or 'yantras' is a very powerful means of internalizing the many forces that make up the Seven Sacred Seals. Each Seal will awaken different forces and archetypes in your psyche. Using your intuition, you may wish to create visual representations of the inner forces and arrange them in harmonic patterns using sacred geometry or inspired artwork. Such art can then become a part of your own inner visualization and embodiment practice, as you allow it to enter more and more deeply into your heart, mind and soul.

THE VENUS SEQUENCE

It is strongly recommended that you use the Transmission of the Seven Sacred Seals alongside the Venus Sequence. As you work with your Venus Sequence, you will soon see why and how these two teachings dovetail. When you begin the Venus Sequence, you can use the prayers and practices in this book alongside the Seventh Seal, and afterwards, as your awareness of your Sequence deepens, you can bring in the other six Seals. In this way you will be making use of both the evolutionary current through the Venus Sequence, and the involutionary current of the Seven Sacred Seals.

TEARS OF GRACE

One of the most blessed of experiences is to receive a spontaneous visitation from the spirit of Grace. Whatever form this may take in your life, it is to be deeply treasured. Manifestations of Divine Grace inevitably evoke soft streams of tears to fall from our eyes as our heart peals open to encompass the depth of the gratitude we feel. Such tears are magical as they are imbued with the quintessence of the Grace. You can collect these tears and imbue any object or article of clothing with them. They are a blessing that carries untold magical telesmic currents. Objects imbued with such tears will forever carry Grace into the lives and homes of those who bear them, as well as generating a ring of protective pure light around us. You are therefore encouraged to gather the tears of Grace and use them as your heart guides you.

THE SEVEN SACRED SEALS

PART 4

THE SEVEN INVOCATIONS

INVOCATION OF THE SEVENTH SEAL

GENE KEY	–	22ND
SIDDHI	–	Grace
STAR	–	Sirius
QUALITY	–	Gathering
ARCHANGEL	–	Tsaphkiel
WOUND	–	The World Wound
I CHING LINE	–	All Lines
SUBTLE BODY	–	The Monadic

PRIME TEACHING

Suffering is Grace

*W*E *begin this Invocation with the*
blessing of the Five Elements.

Angel of Earth, please purify my physical body

Angel of Water, please purify my astral body

Angel of Air, please purify my mental body

Angel of Fire, please sanctify my spirit

Angel of Ether, please gather the quintessence

INVOCATION OF THE SEVENTH SEAL

*B*EINGS *of the Pure Light and the Holy Higher worlds,*
we stand here before you in communion and reverence.

We lift up our hearts and hold our minds pure for the duration
of this Invocation.

We seek to align ourselves with the highest harmonies
and frequencies of intelligence and light, that they may pierce us
to the core of our being, opening us to the arch of the infinite,
and coaxing us softly into the arms of our essence.

> *We come to invoke the Seventh Divine Ray,*
> *that we may partake of its Grace.*
> *We come before you naked and vulnerable, with all our wounds,*
> *our mistakes and our past karma visible and transparent.*
> *We hide nothing from the Great Light.*
> *We open our hearts, our minds and our bodies to you.*
> *We offer you every living cell and atom.*
> *We offer you our desires, our dreams,*
> *our longings, our Holy intention.*
> *We offer you our Gifts, our talents,*
> *our Siddhis, our Divine Genius.*
> *We offer you our pain, our loss, our forgetting, our fear.*
> *We offer you our sadness, our anger, our lust, our selfishness,*
> *our denial, our shame, our cruelty,*
> *our guilt and our indifference.*

Especially we lay before you these many challenges of our
humanity, for your transmutation.

We lay our mortality before you.

We lay our life before you and come to you once again
as a young child, a sweet innocent infant —
before fear, before hope, before suffering.

We ask for your Divine Grace
to begin dripping into our open, pure heart.
We ask for your Grace to stroke our bodies,
to rustle through the tiny hairs of our skin.
We open our full being to your lustrous, wonderful,
sweetening currents and emanations.

We invoke the shower of Luminescence —
the Holy Light of this Seventh Ray.

We throw our heads up to the sky and open our arms wide
to imbibe the mystery of this inner light.
We let it run softly down our bodies, harmonizing our seven
subtle bodies with its delicate web of woven light.
We breathe in the royal cobalt blue of the luminescent beings,
and their flashing gold scintillae, their blue/gold filaments,
and their soft feminine light alights on us as though the great
Mother herself had placed her sacred blue cloak
upon our shoulders.
We bow deeply to the presence of this Grace, this Holy Shakti
that falls upon us from the celestial realms.
We open our souls to the mystery of the dusk —
to the moments of threshold in our lives.
We embrace the wonder of the fading of the day into night,
as the Holy inner light winds its precious way deeper
and deeper into form and the first stars beckon

and twinkle in the inner sky.
We call it to ourselves, this luminescent light.
We call its wonder and its Grace to go to work in our lives,
to come and live with us, to create hidden passageways
of harmony in the fractal tendrils of our life.
We invite this Luminescence to sparkle our life with miracles,
to open, to enliven, to inspire, to sanctify all those we know, see,
hear, think about and connect to.

We attune ourselves to the light of the star known as Sirius.

The blue/white radiance of an intelligence so far beyond our own
that we cannot yet conceive it.
May this sapphire flame draw us further along our evolutionary curve.
May it shine brighter within our bellies.
May its purifying light shower its great blessings upon every
sentient being here on our earth, Gaia.
May it illuminate the hidden jewels that lie behind our suffering.
May it release the pure light and refine our spiritual perception to
enter into the great mystery
of the holographic Divine Universe.

We bring special attention to the highest of our subtle bodies,
the Monadic Body.

May we come every day closer into communion
with our highest zenith — to be one with the Godhead,
to become a perfect aspect of Deity,
a Divine shard shimmering in the great theatre of the Cosmos.
May our hearts rise up to greet this ineffable,
eternal aspect of our consciousness.

*May we draw this great emanation down step by step
through the six subtle bodies of our aura,
infusing our life at every level with the Divine scent
of intoxicating Truth and numinous Love-Being.*

We are now alive in the stream of the Seventh Ray.

*We feel its super-subtle emanation swirling through our bodies,
touching us in dimensions that we can barely understand.
We give great thanks for this special gift.
We drift in your luminescent heavenly blues and golds.
We allow your inner light to enter our intelligence at whatever
level is suitable to our evolution.
We allow it to find the Divine cracks in our inner world and
filter through the layers, opening us on levels of which we may be
unaware. We smile as your gentle light of Grace opens us to a
higher and higher reality.*

We prepare to receive the great Archangel Tsaphkiel.

*Tsaphkiel — an intelligence surpassing human evolution
a presence of love and bliss so far beyond us . . .
Beneficent life-giving creature of almost unbearable purity.
Great Archangel of Grace,
we surrender all our striving to you.
We surrender all to you.
We court your Divine Grace.
And we surrender not as servants,
but as aspects of your great intelligence
not yet aware of our greater body as you.
We let your sentient heavenly scent flood through us,
filling this room with your exquisite otherworldly aroma.*

Tsaphkiel. We allow you to lift us to a higher plane.
We breathe in your Grace.
We open to its wonders, its mysteries.
In naming you, we allow ourselves to be your conduit,
to be a vessel of Grace.
We affirm to remember you in our lives.
We affirm to work with the currents of the Seven Sacred Seals,
your personal domain of understanding.
We affirm to work with the energy of our suffering.
We understand through your Grace that our suffering
calls us ever closer towards you.
We understand through you that suffering is Grace.
We imbibe this greatest of all human Truths —
Suffering is Grace.
We let this Truth resonate in every cell of our being.
We let our DNA laugh aloud with its Truth.
We are a passage towards the Divine, and our suffering is
the river that leads us finally to the ocean of You, of I Am.

We humbly request the opening of the Seventh Seal.

We know that the opening of such a sacred portal involves a relationship.
We understand that the Seal need only be opened from our side,
remaining as it is permanently open from the higher side
in its infinite compassion.
We also understand that there are no sides,
but that such language serves only as a metaphor
in which the frequencies of Divine Light can be invoked.
We reach out for this opening, with every atom of our consciousness.
We see all our daily desires for what they are —
yearnings for this connection to our greater body.

We pour all those desires that we have towards you,
but we do so without desperation —
We simply long to once again feel the vastness of this love.

We open our wounds to the great Seal.
We accept our individual wound as an aspect of the world wound.
We cradle this sacred wound in the palms of our soul.
We offer it up to you like a hurting child for your healing.
All over the world, we envision others also offering up this same
wound for the sake of the healing of the whole.
We remember the wounds of our ancestors, their fear,
their violence, their grief, their guilt.
In offering you our wound as the world, we offer you
the memories and pain of our ancestors.
We affirm that in working with the Seven Sacred Seals we will come
into closer relationship with our own suffering and our own wound.
We understand that compassion comes from this relationship.
We draw the deep breath of Valour into our lungs and fill them
with your Righteousness. We proffer the wounds of humanity into
the Seventh Sacred Seal.
We do this not as an imaginative exercise, but as an ongoing
commitment to the healing of the whole.

Tsaphkiel, We rejoice in the quality of your inner light
as a gathering point for collective healing.
We rejoice in the Grace that contains and gathers together all
the Seven Rays and their seven streams, their seven lights
and the wounds that they are designed to heal.
We honour the Divine Play in which that which is above
corresponds to that which is below.

*We wonder that every aspect of human suffering has a
corresponding quality of Divine Grace — an intelligence specific
to its healing.
We give great thanks for this perennial teaching of the Seven
Sacred Seals that offers us a language to understand our suffering
and unlock the hidden Grace within it.
We affirm that we are ready to enter into the stream of this Holy
transmission and that we are ready to make space for it
to transform our life.*

*We rejoice that we are standing on the brink of a new World.
We revere the secret beings who are gathered together on the
higher planes to incarnate through us as willing co-participants
in the Great Change, in which humanity will
pass through the fires of purification.
We recognize these teachings as the culmination
of the teachings of Christ, of the Buddha,
and of the ancient Hermetic teachings of Alchemy.
We acknowledge that their primary root, standing behind all,
is the incarnation of the third aspect of the Divine trinity —
the Sacred Feminine, or Holy Spirit.
We prepare ourselves and our world for the coming of such a
group incarnation, for the burgeoning of the field of a collective
consciousness rooted in unconditional love,
unchanging Wisdom and uncompromising Truth.*

*We give great thanks for this secret of the Seven Sacred
Seals and its extraordinary transmission.
We bow our heads to our higher Self.
We allow ourselves time to digest its truths.
We imbibe the exceptional patience necessary
for this great work to come to fruition.*

We bear testament to its authenticity.
We shall continue to open this Seal and to offer our
suffering and that of others into this mystery.

We bring this Invocation to a close
with the Blessing of the Five Elements.

Amen.

INVOCATION OF THE SIXTH SEAL

GENE KEY	-	63rd
SIDDHI	-	Truth
STAR	-	Capella
QUALITY	-	Stilling
ARCHANGEL	-	Gabriel
WOUND	-	Separation
I CHING LINE	-	Line 6
SUBTLE BODY	-	The Atmic

PRIME TEACHING

Truth is Surrender

*W*E *begin this Invocation with the blessing of the Five Elements.*

Angel of Earth, please purify my physical body

Angel of Water, please purify my astral body

Angel of Air, please purify my mental body

Angel of Fire, please sanctify my spirit

Angel of Ether, please gather the quintessence

INVOCATION OF THE SIXTH SEAL

*B*EINGS *of the Pure Light and the Holy Higher worlds,*
we stand here before you in communion and reverence.

We lift up our hearts and hold our minds pure for the duration
of this Invocation.

We seek to align ourselves with the highest harmonies
and frequencies of intelligence and light, that they may pierce us
to the core of our being, opening us to the arch of the infinite,
and coaxing us softly into the arms of our essence.

> *We come to invoke the Sixth Divine Ray,*
> *that we may partake of its Divine Truth.*

We prepare ourselves to receive the gentle impact of Truth,
to be open to the holy meaning of the word Truth
and all the Grace it bestows.
We stand before you naked, just as we came into this world,
without boundary or limits, without opinion or knowledge,
without fear or agenda.
The living cells of our body remember this state,
this un-fallen state in which your Presence sang forth from
the atoms of our being in the rapture of your Truth.
We also acknowledge here that as our bodies have grown
and evolved so the seed of the Sacred Wound has caused us
to move further and further from our natural state, and we have
therefore experienced separation from our source.

> *We acknowledge this Separation as our greatest work in life.*
> *We look around ourselves and see the extent and depth*
> *of our separation.*

We humanity have entered a state of forgetting,
a state of removal from that which is eternal.
We wish to acknowledge here the veil that has been drawn
across our eyes, that prevents us from knowing
our true and boundless nature.
We utterly acknowledge the story that has led to this mythical
'Fall from Grace.'
We also acknowledge the perfection of this journey as an aspect
of your Holy Will, your great design.
We even acknowledge the cementing of this story
through the very language of our individuation,
that uses words such as I and You.
We thus use such words now very lightly
in the full knowledge of their falsity.

We offer you our separation.
We offer you the intense agony it causes us.
We acknowledge it as the core reason for our suffering
and the suffering of all who have come before us.
We lay our perceived separation before you
for your Transmutation.

We invoke the exquisite frequency of Quiescence —
the Holy Light of this Sixth Ray.

Such an inner light that it causes our bodies and souls to quiver
with awe as we let it fall upon us, soft as winter snow in a silent,
holy night, like the very night before the Christ is born.
All creatures relapse into silence. Even the rocks bow their
ancient atoms in reverence to the arrival of your Truth.
We breathe softly and deeply and let the silent snow of Truth fall
gently upon our heads, upon our bodies, our hands, our feet.

We allow ourselves to be covered from head to foot.
We feel the freshness of your silence entering our skin,
dissolving into our muscles, sinews, organs.
We feel the Grace of your Truth opening us, healing us, bringing
us slowly back from the dead, cleansing us to the core.

We invoke the mystery of midnight.
We let the snowfall of Truth enter our bones.
We let the crystalline light shine forth from our bones
as each cell of our being recognizes the energy of its source.
We shine like crystal.
We sparkle like snow in starlight.
We radiate with silence, with the silence of utter,
ineffable peace.
We surrender uncontrollably to your peace.
How could we do anything else?

We allow it to go on stilling us, dissolving our fear, dissolving our
separation, bringing us down, melting us, calming us, making our
bodies liquid crystal, quiescent, the light beyond light, the sound
beyond sound, Quietness, Gentleness, Completion, Rest.

We attune ourselves to the light of the star called Capella.

Capella — a golden star, a star of silences, a star of quiescence.
Star of the goat-herder, moving silently through the cosmic sky
with utter focus, utter clarity, keeping all other stars in check.
If the goat-herder's attention wavers, then the goats wander off.
So her attention is dynamic, potent, directing.
It brings stillness and calm to the flock of stars that wander
across the vaults of the heavens.

*Capella — may your stilling light fall upon all
creatures throughout the cosmos.
May the light of your Grace bring peace to earth
and to all sentient beings.*

> *We bring special attention on the vast inner landscape
> of the Atmic Body.
> The Sixth dimensional layer of our being.
> The Divine Mind.
> The inner space of silence.*

*May we come each day into deeper attunement with the beauty
of this 'no-mind' — this eternal mind of brilliance,
bursting with potential, with possibility.
May we come into the ground of our Truth as this pregnant inner
silence out of which all our thoughts,
stories and evolutions flow.
May we rest here in our deep being, no matter which story is
unwinding on the surface of our lives.
May the Truth of this infinite mind of the Atmic Body
inform our every thought, word and deed.
May we settle daily into its endless peace,
living with the vast trust in all life that it brings us.*

> *We are now alive in the stream of the Sixth Ray.*

*We allow our bodies to rock gently as the extraordinary simplicity
of Truth floods through us.
If ever we have felt afraid of the higher frequencies,
of the vastness of our true nature,
let us be reminded here in the Quiescent realm of Truth,
of the sheer easiness of Divine Grace.*

Let us give our thanks for such a gift.
Let us imprint our cells, our living DNA with this memory,
this inner reference point for what Truth truly is.
It has no fight or resistance in it.
It is utter surrender — the absence of resistance.
It is Love — love as silence, love as softness, love as nothingness,
love as everythingness.
May it surround us forever,
may it emanate from within us.
May it bring us back home.

We prepare to receive the great Archangel Gabriel.

An intelligence close to the Godhead itself.
An intelligence of such beauty and purity that were we
afforded the Grace to see it, our souls would instantly
burst into the infinite light of their essence.
Gabriel, great Archangel of Truth, you have appeared
before us before, in many guises —
touch us now with your essence.

Lay your shining feminine hand upon our furrowed brows.
Dissolve our worries and our woes,
recalibrate our hearts to your Truth.
Smile your compassionate smile within us.
Let us merge our consciousness with yours,
Oh being of infinite graciousness and generosity,
Let us enter into communion with you —
our greater being, in silence.
Let us taste daily the endless drifts of the wisdom of your silence
— our inheritance, our birthright.

Let us reclaim that which we have long forgotten,
and let us share it with the world, with our brothers and sisters,
with all creatures on this beautiful world.

Gabriel, we need not yearn for our Truth.
We need only let go and it will be there.
This is your testament — that Truth is Surrender.
We imbibe this vast unparalleled human Truth.
We let it emanate from within the core structure of our DNA.
We hum with it. We resound with its simple silence.
Truth is Surrender.
Our work is separation from God.
You are our great guide working within us, inseparable from us,
reminding us always of the beyond. Reminding us always of the
simplicity that comes from surrender to that which is.

We humbly request the opening of the Sixth Seal.

Our souls reach out to the threshold of our higher consciousness
— the Divine Mind — as pure as crystal,
a mind that spans all time, that dissolves space, the mind that
repairs the great rent in the fabric of our being, that shows us
directly the Truth of our union with all.
We seek to retrieve this aspect of our soul that has fallen out of union.
We seek to receive Divine Truth into the heart of our being, into
the millions of phosphate crystals that make up the DNA in every
cell of our body.

We open our Wound of separation
and offer it into this great Sixth Seal.
We understand that humanity once lived in a merged field —
that in a faraway epoch our consciousness knew itself as light,

as love, beyond time and space.
We understand that our falling into the dense field of matter was
no punishment meted out for sins.
We understand that there was never any fall from Grace.
Grace has forever remained while our consciousness buried itself
deeper into form, forgetting its Holy origin.
We understand the perfection of this process and we give infinite
thanks for the stage we are now in the great game of life.
We bow to the Truth that is returning to humanity.
We tremble with anticipation for the great event, the Great
Change, the transitionary era that is upon us, that is coming closer
every day — as consciousness unveils itself to return to its origin.
We bear witness to the suffering of our world.
We feel it keenly in our every cell.
We feel the weight of our suffering and the anguish we have
continued to propagate through this separation.
It is through the Sixth Seal that the light of Truth
is returning to the world.

When Christ spoke the immortal words
    'I am the Way, the Truth and the Light,'
he was giving voice to the opening of this portal of memory.
We each are the Way, the Truth and the Light.
We each are the Christ, the bearer of the Sacred Wound
of Separation, of indifference and forgetting.
And the Christ is the presence of the eternal 'I'
that heals this wound.
We know ourselves as the Christ light.
We surrender our world, and the suffering of all in it,
into the Great Seal.
We invoke the opening of this Sixth Seal
and the permanent dispelling of the illusion of our separation.

We rejoice at the beauty of our incarnation.
We allow our fullest incarnation to occur.
We revel in the power of the inner light of Quiescence
as it breaks open our form and streams forth from our every atom
as Light and Truth.
We invoke the highest siddhic frequencies from the heavenly
realms to come and live in us, to purify us,
to raise our consciousness onto the higher planes, and to bring
those higher planes and ground them in the earth of our lives.
Let everything and everyone that we touch, look at, think of,
feel the breath of Truth opening and expanding in their lives.

We give great thanks for this secret teaching of the Seven Sacred
Seals, and we embrace its living transmission within our lives.
We vow inwardly to work with these higher currents and forces,
to prepare the soil of our lives for the great incarnations of Truth
that are coming.
We feel the stilling of our wandering energies,
the coming to fruition of all our incarnations.
We sense and anticipate the great feast that is being prepared,
as the Divine Synarchy, the Fellowship of Light,
enters the stream of the three lower worlds and brings with it
utter transformation and Grace.

We bring this Invocation to a close
with the Blessing of the Five Elements.

Amen.

INVOCATION OF THE FIFTH SEAL

GENE KEY	–	4TH
SIDDHI	–	Forgiveness
STAR	–	Vega
QUALITY	–	Diffusing
ARCHANGEL	–	Tsadkiel
WOUND	–	Guilt
I CHING LINE	–	Line 5
SUBTLE BODY	–	The Buddhic

PRIME TEACHING

Forgiveness is Freedom

*W*E *begin this Invocation with the blessing of the Five Elements.*

Angel of Earth, please purify my physical body

Angel of Water, please purify my astral body

Angel of Air, please purify my mental body

Angel of Fire, please sanctify my spirit

Angel of Ether, please gather the quintessence

INVOCATION OF THE FIFTH SEAL

*B*EINGS *of the Pure Light and the Holy Higher worlds,*
we stand here before you in communion and reverence.

We lift up our hearts and hold our minds pure for the duration
of this Invocation.

We seek to align ourselves with the highest harmonies
and frequencies of intelligence and light, that they may pierce us
to the core of our being, opening us to the arch of the infinite,
and coaxing us softly into the arms of our essence.

> *We come to invoke the Fifth Divine Ray,*
> *that we may partake of its Grace.*

In entering into sacred dialogue with this Seal we bow our heads
and open our hearts to receive its special teaching concerning
karma, fate and forgiveness.
We acknowledge here the inner mystery of human destiny —
the hidden reasons for the events of the outer world,
of why people suffer in their various ways, of why some are
granted worldly success and others not, of the Divine timing
behind events, behind birth and death.
It is through the light of this Fifth Seal that the forces that drive
karma are both understood and released.
We acknowledge the Wounds of our ancestors
that are carried in our bloodlines.
We acknowledge the specific purpose for our personal wounds
in offering us the opportunity for Grace.
We also acknowledge the specific purpose of humanity's collective
Wounds in offering us all the opportunity to experience Grace.

*We openly accept our ancestral wounds
as the expression of our cosmic guilt.
This guilt is not intended as punishment for past transgressions.
Rather it is the natural working out of our collective past through the
vehicles of the present, our lower bodies. We each carry a residue of
such guilt, hidden deeper than our conscious mind can comprehend.
We know and acknowledge here that our life is the working out of this
karma, this Cosmic Guilt, and as such it is precious beyond measure.*

*We enter now into the inner hall where our store of guilt lives.
We openly embrace it, whatever form it may take.
We know that within its denseness lies a great shining jewel
— our forgiveness.
We know that we must forgive ourselves for everything we have done.
We know that nothing is hidden from the invisible world
— that our every thought, desire and intent is recorded
in our subtle bodies.
We offer you our mistakes, our flaws, our misunderstandings.
We offer you the depth of our imperfection,
past, present and future.
We lay our ancestral and personal karma before you
for your Transmutation.*

*We invoke the frequency of Pearlescence —
the Holy Light of this Fifth Ray.*

*Mysterious diffusing light. Secret light. Hidden Light of precious
gems beneath the earth, of subterranean light of unknown
caverns. Flowing light of the inside of shells,
of pearls beneath the sea, of mother-of-pearl enclosed in silent
shells, unseen by eyes.*

Pearlescence.

Silver-grey softness awash with the swishing of the dark green sea.
Pearlescent light, reflected light, faraway light.
Stars beneath the ocean, the brushing sounds of the crystal
creatures that live in the ocean deeps.
Forgiving light, diffusing light, swaying breath of light that washes
the soils of our souls, softening our hearts with its ease.

We let the light of Pearlescence ring through our cells.
We invite its silent glint into our bones.
We feel it inside us.
We have forgotten that it lives inside us this hidden light,
this forgotten light, this treasure sought by so many.

We invoke the beauty of all hidden light.
Light that lies concealed from the eye.
Light so subtle and soft that it washes past us unseen.
We dive now into this hidden pearly world.
We wash our souls in its light of forgiveness.
We give ourselves the gift of forgiveness.
We give the world our gift of forgiveness.
We surrender our awareness — our heart, body,
mind into the diffusing light of Forgiveness,
and we let it wipe us clean.

We float softly down into the gracious depths of this
quintessence, and as we drop, so in turn we feel lighter.
The deeper we drop, the lighter we feel.

We attune ourselves to the light of the star Vega.

Vega, spectral blue/white star,
ancient polestar of our un-fallen epoch.
One day in the far future you will again be our polestar,
our guiding light, and your subtle light will bring our evolution
to its final close, as we enter the Age of Eternity.
Vega — fifth brightest star in the heavens
Star of fives, star of the quintessence, star of the weaver,
star of the lyre, of Orpheus the Divine Bard.
May your soft, lilting music coax us to sleep and while we dream
may our souls be washed clean by your light of Divine Forgiveness.
Sweet Vega, may your soft light be known by all beings on earth,
and may we all surrender to your wonderful Grace.

We bring special attention to the fifth subtle body — the Buddhic Body
Our body of ecstasy, our higher solar radiance,
our feminine Divine heart.
May our self-forgiveness ripple through the caverns of our being,
releasing the old wounds, the stored-up, pent-up karma.
May our hearts open to swim in the luscious currents and
emanations of our Bliss Body, this great body of compassion.
May our hearts bleed red into the sea of creation.
May the Red Buddha sweep us clean.

We are now alive in the stream of the Fifth Ray.

We give thanks for the special gift of this Holy essence of Forgiveness.
Such a liquid truth it is, slushing through our body, eroding,
stroking, releasing, massaging, opening, deepening our breath
as it moves and flows through our body.
May this soothing balm be present in us all.

*May its silk, soft coils become the breath of our days and ground
of our endless lives.*

> *We prepare to receive the great Archangel Tsadkiel.*

*Angel of Mercy. Angel of Martyrs, of the bravest souls.
Angel who smiles and loves above all those who are willing
to sacrifice the small for the sake of the whole.
Tsadkiel, great balancer, smoother of all rough edges,
eroder of karma and retainer of karma.
We bow to your deep justice — we bow to the Grace
inherent in your sacred contracts with us.
You who match our frequency to the karma we are capable
of transforming in life.
You who stretch us, who waits for us to see through the veil,
who encourages us to make the transition from the life of the
small to the life of the great.*

*Tsadkiel, we bow deeply to your infinite mercy —
to the sweet aroma of your forgiveness.
We breathe in your perfume.
We let the subtle pearlescent emanation fill this space around us.
We inhale you.
We recognize this aroma from some distant place just beyond our
reach — it is the aroma of wholeness passing through the Seal
as it opens...*

> *We humbly request the opening of the Fifth Seal.*

*We inhale again that pure delicate aroma of forgiveness,
the great Siddhi that travels backwards through time.
It is the essence of the risen Christ, working its mystical passage
through our DNA, tunnelling backwards through the illusion of time*

and space, clearing and forgiving — debts, wrongs, wounds, curses
— drawing out hooks, unwinding ancestral ties between people,
tribes, races, dimensions — always returning essence to its source,
always reconciling, always rebalancing, always opening our hearts
wider and wider, freeing our bodies of unconscious burdens and
patterns, personal and ancestral baggage, emotional wounds, past
hurts and resentments, pain and anguish, rage, blame and grief.
We surrender our karma — our baggage, our burden, our guilt —
into the Fifth Seal that was closed to our race once upon a time
long, long ago.

We now implore you to reopen this Seal and let the healing
currents of our vast love come bursting and exploding through
the narrow neck into the present moment.
The future meeting the past.
Grace meeting suffering, transmuting it, fusing it,
merging with it in the cauldron of our bellies and our bodies.
We offer ourselves up into this Fifth Seal — we become the sacrificial
lamb for the currents of wonder, the Divine currents of forgiveness.
We see that one day, this emanation, this Siddhi, will sweep
humanity clean, will reset all our wounding, will release all
karmic debt at every level, and thus will it lead to the great wind
of Freedom that will dance through the world.

Tsadkiel, great Archangel of Balance, let the wind of your justice
lift us on the wings of your world.
A world in which that which is above reflects that which is below,
in perfection.
It is through us, through our loves, our ties, our relationships
that you offer us the harvest of the whole.
You offer us Union, you offer us perfect love, love with Freedom,
love unconditional. May your Grace bring us closer to our deep

allies, our brothers and sisters.
May your Grace free us from all ancestral anguish.
May it lead to the dawn of the new relationships, the Divine
Lovers, the Holy couples, the alchemical wedding of opposites,
to create vast fields of harmony, of beauty, of love.

Forgiveness is Freedom.

With these simple words we lay the foundation of a whole new
world — a world without fear, a world of friendship,
a world of ease based on a Trust beyond all understanding,
a Trust that cannot be broken,
because the Trust contains forgiveness within it at all moments.
We surrender to this great Truth — Forgiveness is Freedom.

We rejoice in the coming of this Siddhi of Forgiveness into the world.
It comes as the hand of Grace at the appointed hour according
to the secret laws.
May we enact it in our daily lives, in our relationships,
in our worldview.
May it bring us a new level of tolerance and compassion towards
those in whom the Siddhi is not yet aware of itself.
May it soften our gaze and at the same time renew our zeal
to help those in need.
May this Siddhi of Forgiveness spread in our attitude to life,
and inspire others with its subtle emanation.
Whomever carries this Holy Gift of Forgiveness, let him or her be
blessed by the highest of all blessings, and let them be an agent of
Grace wherever they go in this world or the next.

We give great thanks for this secret teaching
of these Seven Sacred Seals.

We realise that to work with such energies
is a great privilege only given to a few.
We receive the honour with all our heart in the knowledge
that we will pass it on through our daily lives, to our friends,
our families, our allies, even our enemies.
We revel in the pearly gates of the heavenly world,
and we stand willing as a channel for such a gift of Grace.

Let Forgiveness and Freedom rule in the world.

We bring this Invocation to a close with the
Blessing of the Five Elements.

Amen.

INVOCATION OF THE FOURTH SEAL

GENE KEY	-	43ᴿᴰ
SIDDHI	-	Epiphany
STAR	-	Alderbaran
QUALITY	-	Catalyzing
ARCHANGEL	-	Haniel
WOUND	-	Rejection
I CHING LINE	-	Line 4
SUBTLE BODY	-	The Causal

PRIME TEACHING

We are the Epiphany

*W*E *begin this Invocation with the blessing of the Five Elements.*

Angel of Earth, please purify my physical body

Angel of Water, please purify my astral body

Angel of Air, please purify my mental body

Angel of Fire, please sanctify my spirit

Angel of Ether, please gather the quintessence

INVOCATION OF THE FOURTH SEAL

*B*EINGS *of the Pure Light and the Holy Higher worlds,*
we stand here before you in communion and reverence.

We lift up our hearts and hold our minds pure for the duration
of this Invocation.

We seek to align ourselves with the highest harmonies
and frequencies of intelligence and light, that they may pierce us
to the core of our being, opening us to the arch of the infinite,
and coaxing us softly into the arms of our essence.

> *We come to invoke the Fourth Divine Ray,*
> *that we may partake of its Grace.*

This is the Ray of Breakthrough,
a special threshold Ray in which sudden and unexpected
illumination finds its way to earth.
As such, we hold our hearts and minds open to its unknown
mystery — that can create wormholes in our lives.
We also acknowledge here that each of the Seven Sacred Seals
is a corridor leading into and through our hearts,
connecting us with the One Heart, our Divine origin.
When we speak of such love, we shall see that it takes many forms
and styles, just as light itself has many forms and frequencies.
Of these, the Fourth Ray speaks deeply to our humanity,
to our inclusion within the body of humanity.

It calls each of us into the whole, to take our place of warmth
within the fellowship of all beings, around the great council fire
of the elders and those whose consciousness lies far beyond us.

We bow deeply in homage to such beings,
who gather around this Invocation.

We therefore bring to you our human tendency to close off from
the warmth of our fellows, to isolate ourselves through opinion,
habit, low self-esteem and fear of the group.
We bring to you our fear of losing our freedom,
our ancestral stubbornness, our caution before true love,
our impatience with our own innocence and our insensitivity
and intellectual vanity or pride.
We bring before you any quality that keeps us from coming into
the body of humanity, that keeps us on the outside.
We acknowledge the deep grief that all DNA carries, both from
the past horrors and losses, and from our own life wherever we
have failed to honour the voice of our true heart.
We lay before you the layers of numbness that life has placed
upon our chest — the defences we needed as young children
to protect us from hurt, from the wounds of the world.

We bring before you our fear of rejection.
Our habit of forgetting love.
We bring before you the inconsolable sadness of the generations,
the loss of our friends, our families, and our children.
We let the tremor of this heartache in.
We wish to heal our hearts and feel the flow of love once again.
We wish to reconnect to our true mother and rejoin the split
that has crushed and sapped our spirit.
We wish to believe once again in the power of love.
We lay our heart's wounds and the heart's wounds and memories
of our ancestors before you for your Transmutation.

We invoke the frequency of Iridescence —
the Holy Light of this Fourth Ray.

Unusually bright light, fiercely bright,
rainbow kaleidoscope of flickering, fizzing, electrical light.
The light that breaks into our world from the beyond —
the light of the dragonfly's wing, light of the secret mineral realm,
iridescent light that suddenly appears in the dark
and stuns us into silence, into awe.
We feel the charge of Iridescence as it ignites us, ignites in us,
as it sizzles around us, penetrates us, trembling and quaking
and snaking around the base of our spine,
enlivening all deadness, shocking numbness into life,
bursting our dullness into living flames.
We relax deeper as the iridescent light spirals up our spine,
opening its links, targeting pain, targeting blockages, magnetized
by heavy spaces, tornado-ing through our sinew and muscle
and bone, opening our energy body,
bridging the realms of physical, astral, mental.

We allow your Iridescent Grace to spin within us, to visit every
corner and crevice of our being, to seek out our pain,
our long forgotten baggage.
We cannot help but feel enthused.
We cannot help but be awakened,
revivified by this light of Epiphany.
We cannot help but be inspired, illuminated,
refreshed, moved, provoked into action out of stasis.
We embrace the quickening that this light of Iridescence
inevitably brings in its wake. We invoke it,
we long for this life force, this youthful inextinguishable vigour.
Ah, how blissful we feel when your smile touches us this deeply.

We attune ourselves to the light of the star Aldebaran.

Aldebaran — great orange giant of the firmament.
Sacred keeper of the seven sisters, eye of the bull, loosed arrow
of the sacred hunter. Your reddening beauty falls upon our
people with intensity, with unparched zeal, and drawing us ever
inwards, you pour your vast heart-light into our souls.
We invoke your bright eye, we receive your wicked smile,
we humanity give ourselves up to your Divine passion.
We ask that your light pierce and penetrate the dark places in our
world of form, that your orange lasers awaken the dark places in
our souls, catalysing us, quickening us,
speeding up our evolution.

We receive your vastness.
We breathe in your electrical intensity.
We surrender to the power of your intense Grace.

We bring special attention to the fourth subtle body,
the Causal Body.

Our body of illumination, our entry-point into the hidden
mysteries, our first contact with the inner light.
We celebrate the great mystery of incarnation,
of the purity that we have gathered down the Aeons,
that we have stored in our Causal Body.
We attune to our Causal body — that immortal soul that travels
through the ages, that is the conduit of all higher forces,
of all our greatest moments, of all that is good and pure in our lives.

We are now alive in the stream of the Fourth Ray.

We give thanks for the special gift
of this magical light of Epiphany.
We bow as children to the myriad miraculous ways in which
Grace can move in our lives. We acknowledge the perfection
of the phase of our life we are moving through.
We acknowledge the perfection of the incarnation
we are currently moving through.
We deeply honour every present moment we travel through.
May the potent catabolic energy of the Fourth Ray shine forth in
the hearts of all creatures in all universes.

We prepare to receive the great Archangel Haniel.

Haniel, iridescent feminine spirit of laughter and joy —
great healer of sadness,
compassionate embodiment of Divine empathy.
We surrender to your lightness,
to the beauty and softness in your eyes.
We offer you our love, such as it is, that you may augment it,
that you may fan its flames into a glittering crescendo of joy
and hope and peace.
Haniel, we remain always open to your lightest touch —
we invite breakthrough in our lives.
We invite your Epiphany — that rushing charge of light
as it swells and hurtles inside us to reform our lives,
to reshape our destiny, to reinvigorate our spirit.

We humbly request the opening of the Fourth Seal.

We lie before you as children, as the baby Jesus lay in his crib,
awaiting his Epiphany — his crowning.
We imbibe the great power of this symbolic truth,

the mystery of our christening, of our Epiphany,
overseen by the wise ones, by our inner guides,
our personal Magi, who guard and protect our essence
as we grow through life.
We surrender our numbness, our deafness into the Seal.
We ask for the sparkling light of Epiphany to visit our lives.
We let go of caring or worrying about the timing
of our Epiphanies, our initiations.
We smile and trust in the greater plan,
in its timing, in its perfection.

We anchor ourselves in patience, in the timeless truth.

We pay homage to the awesome gifts that lie hidden behind
this Fourth Seal and its Siddhi of Epiphany.
We understand that one day, in the timing of our world,
this incredible frequency will come pouring into our world,
will destroy all barriers in people's hearts.
It will pave the way for the kingdom of heaven on earth,
an inner state of consciousness in which we no longer
will feel separation as humans.

We await with trust the timing of your great Epiphanies —
we offer our lives as preparation for such numinous events in time.
And we anticipate the next major Epiphany Event,
that will create a collective vessel — a synarchy — for the highest
consciousness to touch down and into the world of form.

We open our hearts into the collective way.
We renew our vows of friendship and trust.
We put our faith in the higher self of humanity —
to love itself, our world and all the creatures and forms

who live beside us.
We model this new way in our lives,
in our families, at work and in the world.
We are the Epiphany.
This is the core Truth.
Not you, or I or he or she or them,
but We.
We are the Epiphany.

It is our heart, together, as one, that leads us into the next phase
of our evolution. There will be no I.

We rejoice in the coming of this extraordinary Siddhi
of Epiphany into the world.
We the fellowship, we the synarchy,
open our lives to receive a higher Truth.
We embrace a world with boundaries but no borders,
with difference but no judgement, with change but no pain.
We invoke the great Siddhi of Epiphany.
We plant it as a seed in our inner life.
As we work to purify our consciousness, through aligning to our
purpose, through compassionate action in our relationships
and through service to the whole,
so we open ourselves to the power of Epiphany.
May it fall on us when we least expect it.
May it come when we need it the most, may it break open
our hearts, heal our bodies and expand our minds.
May it jump from us to our neighbour.
May it jump from our neighbour to the community.
May it ripple out into the body of humanity, releasing hurt,
letting the healing balm of tears fall from our eyes to cleanse
our souls and open the way for a new world.

We give great thanks for this secret teaching
of these Seven Sacred Seals.
We let it become a pattern woven into our lives,
a new fabric that unravels within us, leading us forward
with great clarity into the challenges that lie ahead.

> *We acknowledge that we are heading into turbulent times*
> *of great change.*
> *We take a deep breath and nod our knowing*
> *as we gaze into this Seal.*
> *Epiphany is Initiation.*
> *It comes when it comes,*
> *and when it comes it creates shock.*
> *It creates vast, unprecedented change.*
> *And it also comes for the benefit of all.*
> *We prepare ourselves for this future.*
> *We prepare humanity, we prepare those who are ready to listen,*
> *for the shocks that will one day rock our world.*

We let the light of the inner worlds guide our every decision,
and we trust absolutely in the Grace of the teachings that come to
prepare us to meet our glorious Epiphany.

> *We bring this Invocation to a close*
> *with the Blessing of the Five Elements.*

Amen.

INVOCATION OF THE THIRD SEAL

GENE KEY	-	25TH
SIDDHI	-	Love
STAR	-	Regulus
QUALITY	-	Radiating
ARCHANGEL	-	Raphael
WOUND	-	Shame
I CHING LINE	-	Line 3
SUBTLE BODY	-	The Mental

PRIME TEACHING

Love Ends Suffering

WE begin this Invocation with the blessing of the Five Elements.

Angel of Earth, please purify my physical body

Angel of Water, please purify my astral body

Angel of Air, please purify my mental body

Angel of Fire, please sanctify my spirit

Angel of Ether, please gather the quintessence

INVOCATION OF THE THIRD SEAL

*B*EINGS *of the Pure Light and the Holy Higher worlds,*
we stand here before you in communion and reverence.

We lift up our hearts and hold our minds pure for the duration
of this Invocation.

We seek to align ourselves with the highest harmonies
and frequencies of intelligence and light, that they may pierce us
to the core of our being, opening us to the arch of the infinite,
and coaxing us softly into the arms of our essence.

> *We come to invoke the Third Divine Ray,*
> *that we may partake of its Grace.*

We wonder at the mystery of the Seven Sacred Seals and their
hidden pathways and practices.
We acknowledge the wonders of the manifestations of Grace as it
opens up the ventricles of our hearts to the light of luminescence.
Within this tapestry woven of light, we come to embrace
the Third Holy Ray and its emanation of Universal Love.
Here we come to capture this quintessence that hides in the heart
of every human being.
Here in the Third Ray we come to the most universal Ray —
the Ray of Love.
All are Rays of Love, but the Third Ray is the love within all forms.
It is the essence of love waiting to be released from its vehicle.
All forms are vehicles for transporting and transmitting love.
Even love that is not love is still love.

We invoke the mystery of our sacred wound.
We hold aloft our human shame.
We do not know. We did not realise.
We are lost. We did not mean to.
We are hurting so deeply because of it.
We are sorry. We are so sorry.
Please help us. Please hear us.
We place our human faults at your feet.
We place our failures and our struggles at your feet.
We kneel before you helpless.
We have nothing. We are nothing.
We are everything. We are you. You are us.
There is no blame.
We accept our shame as the patina of our learning.
We grow through our pain.
We learn from our mistakes.
We know that there are mistakes and there are no mistakes.
Our shame is not a mistake. It is your voice inside us
wishing for union, remembering something better,
something higher.

We bring before you our shame.
We carry the shame of the whole and we ought to feel it.
It is for our healing.
It does not diminish us when we accept it absolutely.
It becomes us.
We become greater through this acceptance.
We bring before you our tendency to pass the buck,
to try and wriggle out of our responsibility.
We would rather not take on the burdens of the world.
We would rather hide away from all this pain.
We bring before you our fear of commitment.

We bring before you all our human weakness.
We bring before you our addiction to the drama,
to the many distractions of the outer life.
We offer you our desire for pleasure.
We offer you our selfishness, cultivated when we were young.
We bring before you our arrogance and vanity,
to think that we have any control whatsoever.
We lay all these wounds and cries and shames
before you for your Transmutation.

We invoke the frequency of Rubescence —
the Holy Light of this Third Ray.

Rubescence is the red/gold light of love,
the light of life as it radiates the form.
We bow to this warmth of life, the life-giving light,
this inextinguishable light.
We look to the sun for the model of Rubescence —
of the solar fire, the cosmic fire, the radiant aurora of your love.
We draw your flames, your sacred flames deep into the crucibles
of our cells, we fan the flames of your love as it melts our shame,
as it warms the cockles of our hearts, as it brings release and
smiles and laughter and humour into the breath we breathe
into our bodies.
We dream of this red gold light — this rose within the core of all life.
We draw in its fiery memory, its soft hearth of royal crimson.
We revel in its reverence.
We sigh to the base of our spine with its hearty wine-red warmth.

We invite the warmth of Rubescence — the halo of every God
and the rosy cheeks of every Goddess to soften us,
to moisten us, to bring us back to life.

We kindle the flames of our longing, of our sweet innocent longing
to run and cavort and bound across the fields of life, without the
heaviness, without the weight of our shame. Rubescence, you are
the light of serious laughter,
of strict playfulness, of penniless royalty,
of the freedom of flight, of the flight of feet with wings,
of the gold in the green, the red gold hidden in the green of our world,
and the glistening love that flecks our eyes,
that releases our sighs and echoes in the skies...

    We attune ourselves to the light of the star Regulus.

Regulus, the bountiful, the mighty, the King,
Regulus the centre, the heart of the lion, The Cor Leonis.
Star of vast heat, star of royalty,
we invoke your light and draw your flames into our eyes.
We open our eyes and draw your golden light into our eyes.
And we let your gold come deeper down into our throats,
into our voices, into our chests, down into our bellies
where the whirlpool of your love kindles our own great love.
For we are each royal.
We are each a King or Queen — Regent of Everything,
Ruler of Nothing.
Let your light become a red giant in our belly, let it grow
and grow until we can no longer contain your love, your healing.
Until it bursts forth from within us in countless rings upon rings
of warmth, of miles upon miles of smiles, the echoing laughter
of the Buddhas, of the joke, of the great joke.
Ah yes, Regulus, how you bless us with the mischief of your smile,
your warm blooded touch of your deeply loving Grace.
    We bring special attention to the third subtle body —
    the mental body.

Our body of magic. Our mind that only attracts —
attracts thoughts, forms, subtle forms, forms that live with us,
that adhere to us — forms that diminish us and forms
that expand us.
It is here through our minds, our greatest magical allies —
that we have the power to know love.
How can our minds love, we may sometimes wonder?
Because our minds contain the whole.
Our minds expand beyond the body, out into the vastness of space.
Our mind is a reflection of the great void.
We give thanks for our mental body, our mind, that draws in
the forces of light, that attracts and amasses our good fortune,
that transforms lead into gold.
The mind of love is the mind that sees love everywhere,
in all people, in all things.
Even in nothing can the loving mind find the wellspring of love.

We are now alive in the stream of the Third Ray.

We give thanks for the special gift of this bounteous light
of Universal Love.
We attune ourselves to the light of dawn,
the golden orb of the sun rising out of the earth, the fresh song
of the birds and the first subtle movements of the tiny creatures
just before the dawn.
Everything is moving, everything is awakening.
Everything is filled to bursting with love.
We swim and dive through the stream of the Third Ray.
Like the otter at play, we whirl and spin and gambol
and then we lie and dry ourselves naked in the sun while the
gentle breeze of your Grace plies its spring fingers in our shining
hair.

We prepare to receive the great Archangel Raphael.

Archangel Raphael, great Angel of healing and love.
We bow to receive your bursting emerald gold heart.
We feel the gentle play of your vibrations as your emanation
brings us into the sphere of Grace.
You are the very heart of Grace.
Your presence fills a great city, so wide is your reach.
Your love touches the edges of the known, and draws its endless
nourishment from the depths of the unknown.
Blessed by God are you great Raphael, blessed to carry the love
of God and to beam it into our lives — to heal our ills, to burn
out old wounds and memories with your rose gold flames.
Archangel of the people are you Raphael.
So many times the one we call upon, knowing or unknowing.
Answerer of prayers, giver of blessings, granter of invocations,
inspirer of dreams.
You live close to us all, you live right within our hearts.
Let us be filled with your presence, your easiness,
your relaxedness, with the rosy aura of your endless love,
given by God.

We humbly request the opening of the Third Seal.

We understand here the other side of this transmission
of the Seven Sacred Seals.
Here in the third Seal comes the understanding of evil,
and the balancing of the books at the end of days.
For when evil was born, so was shame born,
and so too was human lack.
Here in this Third Seal, we surrender all our selfishness,
born of our fear, driving our greed, born out of ignorance.

*Countless are those who have suffered under the hand of
selfishness, and now the time comes when selfishness will be reaped,
when ignorance will be ended,
when shame will be erased in the radiance of the Divine Sun.
We align ourselves with this reaping, we offer ourselves
up to the flail, to be purified, to be transformed.*

*We allow our souls to be purged,
we allow evil to be driven from our hearts.
We know that our job is not to conquer evil but to understand it.
We ask for this great boon to be gifted in our lives so that we may
live life at its zenith, that we may fulfil our highest purpose,
our utmost destiny of service to the whole.
And we ask for the healing love of Grace to emerge easily
and naturally as our radiance and our purpose.*

*We rejoice at the coming of the Siddhi of Universal Love into the world.
We rejoice that no one and no thing can escape the fiery rays
of this love.
For wherever one hides, there you are.
Whoever you may be, there you are,
beating in the heart of hearts.
We rejoice in the laughter and joy that follows this Siddhi
of Universal Love, that will bring an end to poverty,
that will bring an end to hunger.
We open our hearts and minds to imbibe this vision
of heaven as it dawns on earth.
We know that we need not look to your coming and that all the
saints and masters have always promised your Return.*

*We hold fast to this faith, to this inner certainty of the closing
of the epoch, of the balancing of the books, of the reconciliation*

of the opposites, of the steady resting of consciousness as it populates the form.

> We bear witness to the great Truth of Love —
> that Love ends suffering.
> We soak this Truth into our bones.
> We exude it, we include it,
> we own it at the deepest level in our core.
> Love ends suffering.

We give great thanks for this secret teaching of these Seven Sacred Seals.
We revel in its beauty, in its simplicity, in its mystical power.
We smile deeply with the love that emerges through this Third great Seal, and we hold our hands on our belly in the knowing that we have found the greatest Truth of all — the Truth of Love.

> We bring this Invocation to a close
> with the Blessing of the Five Elements.

Amen.

INVOCATION OF THE SECOND SEAL

GENE KEY	-	17TH
SIDDHI	-	Omniscience
STAR	-	Rigel
QUALITY	-	Penetrating
ARCHANGEL	-	Khamael
WOUND	-	Denial
I CHING LINE	-	Line 2
SUBTLE BODY	-	The Astral

PRIME TEACHING

Omniscience Precedes Transformation

*W*E *begin this Invocation with the*
blessing of the Five Elements.

Angel of Earth, please purify my physical body

Angel of Water, please purify my astral body

Angel of Air, please purify my mental body

Angel of Fire, please sanctify my spirit

Angel of Ether, please gather the quintessence

INVOCATION OF THE SECOND SEAL

*B*EINGS *of the Pure Light and the Holy Higher worlds,*
we stand here before you in communion and reverence.

We lift up our hearts and hold our minds pure for the duration
of this Invocation.

We seek to align ourselves with the highest harmonies
and frequencies of intelligence and light, that they may pierce us
to the core of our being, opening us to the arch of the infinite,
and coaxing us softly into the arms of our essence.

> *We come to invoke the Second Divine Ray,*
> *that we may partake of its Grace.*

We honour here the beautiful distinctiveness between each
of the seven Rays and their specific streams of Grace
and enactment in the world.
Here in this second Ray we find the cool, sharp vision
of intense clarity.
This is the gaze of Grace, the gazing eye of God.
We recall all the legends and myths sown by our ancestors,
of the all-seeing eye, the eye of Horus, the third eye —
that sees directly into God, that God looks through —
to see our lives in a new light, to stir sleeping forces in our minds
and in our hearts — to open our vision to our Divinity.
When working or calling on the Secdond Holy Ray,
we open ourselves to intense inner scrutiny.
Through God's eyes, we come to view where we have come from,
where we have reached, and how far is our goal.

It is through this Divine Second Seal that
we come to see what must be done.
We see the Truth of our spiritual labour, without haze,
or corruption or self-delusion.
This is the great cleansing of sight.
It is the great love that cuts through illusion —
that shows us who we really are.

We bring before you our self delusions, our self grandeur,
our spiritual glamour.
We lay before you our vanity, our proclaimed knowledge,
our opinions, our need to be right, our individuated viewpoint.
We bring before you all the trappings of our denial —
those aspects of our being that prevent us from being the Truth.
We acknowledge the aspects of our proud self
that we cannot see for ourselves.
We acknowledge our blindness, our dumbness,
our holy ignorance.
We lay all our ideas of our holiness before your feet.
We lay our primal anger at your feet.
We lay the rage and blindness of our ancestors at your feet.
We assume responsibility for all violent acts throughout time,
as we ourselves have been violent, either in our thoughts,
in our self judgments, in our attitude towards others
and sometimes in our actions.
We bring all that is hidden from our own sight
before you for your Transmutation.

We surrender everything to the eye of God —
that it may cleanse us and open us up to the Truth.

We invoke the frequency of Phosphorescence —
the Holy Light of this Second Ray.
We acknowledge that our DNA,
the bedrock of our being,
sits upon a backbone of phosphates,
tiny chemical bonds,
whose very name means to shine out with inner light.

We note the two different qualities present in phosphorescence
— the shining gentleness of the many in the one, and the fiercely
penetrating gaze of the hunter of Truth.

At night on a moonlit sea,
when the wind drops and the stars dance their glittering czardas
in the deep blue sky,
sometimes we may look down and see the phosphorescence.
The countless millions of tiny sea creatures,
a mirror of the heavens,
shining their silent truth back at the stars. And this light,
this connective light, between sea and stars, between the tiny
and the vast, the ocean and the drop — this is the quality and
texture of phosphorescence.
Let us feel now how the web of the cosmos is stitched together in
the fabric of an order so perfect that we can hardly hold
that vision in our daily lives.

We open to receive the holographic truth of the
interconnectedness of all beings, of all moments, of all things.
And within this fabric, this holy canopy, we invite the other side
of the eye — the eye of Truth to see through us.
When this eye opens, it opens suddenly.
It may shock us and make us feel uncomfortable.

We accept this discomfort as an aspect of your Grace at work.
Phosphorescence, burning through us,
like its element in name — phosphorous.
A light so brief and bright that it will change us forever.
All the brightness of the entire cosmos focused into one tiny spot,
one tiny instant - the place of our blindness.
May the holy light of phosphorescence find our blind spot,
illuminate it so sharply with its white-hot heat
that we may never again be blind to ourselves.

We attune ourselves to the light of the star Rigel.

Great Blue Supergiant, lying at the foot of Orion,
the cosmic hunter. It is your gaze that seals our fate.
We invoke your inconceivable brightness.
We invoke it within the caverns of our brain.
Deep inside us you burn, etching your inner light as phosphenes,
as sacred scripts, as burning letters,
magical sigils of fire bursting across our neural net.
You Rigel, the connector, the wizard, the seer, the hierophant.
May your skies open up within us, to allow us to see the greater
vision, to know and embody the vastness of our role as gods, as deity.
Shine in our brain, and shine in our heart, stitching the two
together, for as our mind opens, so does our heart,
and as our heart opens, so does our mind.
We pay homage to Thoth, to Hermes Trismegistus,
great collective being who sowed the star seed
deep within human DNA before the fabled Fall.
We reach out to you, to trigger our memory,
through your language of light, your sacred fire letters,
your cellular keys, your Gene Keys.

We bring special attention to the second subtle body,
the astral body.

Our astral nature, two sided, two-headed —
shunning pain on one side and seeking pleasure on the other.
Desire.
Residue and dumping ground for ancestral karma.
Every emotion is a life within us. Every feeling, every emotional
charge behind every thought, word and deed carries our karma,
imprints our DNA. Thus we cycle endlessly drawn back into
our samsara over and over again, to incarnate back into the pain
body, back to the seeker, the quester, the Divine Holy fool.
We ask for this Second great Ray to shine deeply through our
desire nature, to highlight our astral life, the patterns that shape
our dreams, the entities we attract through resonance.
We ask for a clear sight, to see what drives us, what wounds us,
what energy we need to recycle.
We ask for clarity, deep emotional clarity,
so that we know precisely what we must do to renew
our connection to the whole.

We are now alive in the stream of the Second Ray.

We give thanks for this special gift of Omniscience,
of inner sight.

We realise that it can only come to us when we are ready,
when we are committed to God, when we have proven
our resoluteness before the forces of the invisible world.
We affirm to purge and cleanse ourselves of our emotional past,
to heal our wounded inner child,

*to take full responsibility for our feelings and to treat others
with respect and courtesy.
We give up our addiction to conflict, to argumentation,
to all emotional games and battles that stir our wound
and reinforce our misery.
We vow to make use of the vision we are given, to enter a new
cycle in our lives, a cycle of health, of cherishing, of humility.
We begin our life again with a new faith,
a new hope and a new love in our hearts.*

We prepare to receive the great Archangel Khamael.

*Khamael, 'he who sees God' — great being of limitless Sight.
We welcome you into our lives.
We bow deeply to your presence, your omniscient gaze.
It is you who can defeat all evil simply through the compassion
and clarity of your eyes, of your stare.
We ask you Khamael to look into our souls,
to lend us your hawk's vision, to show us
what we most need to see, that place where we cannot yet see.
We ask for your love to fill our lives with vision, to open the eyes
of all our cells, to ignite the presence of Christ within our bodies,
and to drive out those forces that are not in resonance with our
highest vision. Khamael, we vow to work with you, to earn our
view through your eyes, through purification, through spiritual
labour, and above all, through self honesty.*

We humbly request the opening of the Second Seal.

*We realise that we cannot know when this Seal may fully open,
as it depends upon hidden forces that are connected
to the working out of our personal karma.*

*We also realise that when this Seal opens and your Grace pours
through, we will not be the same person that we were before.
We therefore do not ask lightly for the light of your vision.
We ask that you prepare us for the Great Vision with lesser
visions, inner cleanings that help us to live purer lives.*

> *We surrender our denial into this Seal.
> We surrender our irritation, our impatience,
> all our little acts of violence against the whole —
> those unconscious daily patterns that often cause hurt
> to others, directly or indirectly.
> We vow to pay attention to the details, to the tiny,
> to the small moments of our unconsciousness.
> We acknowledge that the great changes are only made
> possible as we learn to address the small changes.
> We vow to learn the intricate pattern that makes up our denial,
> our forgetting.
> We attend to each moment with as much awareness
> as we can bring to bear.*

*We rejoice in the coming of this great Siddhi of Omniscience,
that will reverse the great wound of violence against
humanity and nature.
We understand that it was through this Second Seal
that the sword came into the world, that killing became normal.
We hold the vision of a world without killing,
a world in which no living creature is harmed,
a world that ever was and will one day come again.
We ask that the great Grace of Omniscience fall upon all
those who are capable of deep transformation, of profound self
actualization and we ask that those transformed will lead others
in the same holy direction.*

*We hold fast to the immortal Truth
that Omniscience precedes transformation.
You cannot change without first
seeing the absolute necessity of that change.*

*Therefore we honour Omniscience as one of the most important
of all Siddhis — since it must come,
yet we cannot predict when.
Thus we prepare ourselves for its immanence,
through pure living, through integrity and compassion,
and through deep trusting patience.*

*We give great thanks for this secret teaching
of these Seven Sacred Seals.
We continue to let its profound truths deeper into our bodies,
our hearts and our souls. We need not understand the mysterious
ways in which the transmission enters our lives, but we keep our
faces soft, we stay relaxed in our approach and we breathe
the essence of the wisdom into our core.
We acknowledge that Grace has its timing.
It always waits for a specific moment and a specific place.
We will know when it visits because it will open us from the inside out.
It will peel us open and renew our lives.*

*We bring this Invocation to a close
with the Blessing of the Five Elements.*

Amen.

INVOCATION OF THE FIRST SEAL

GENE KEY	–	40TH
SIDDHI	–	Divine Will
STAR	–	Arcturus
QUALITY	–	Allowing
ARCHANGEL	–	Mikhael
WOUND	–	Repression
I CHING LINE	–	Line 1
SUBTLE BODY	–	The Physical

PRIME TEACHING

We Yield to the Will of the Whole

*W*E begin this Invocation with the
blessing of the Five Elements.

Angel of Earth, please purify my physical body

Angel of Water, please purify my astral body

Angel of Air, please purify my mental body

Angel of Fire, please sanctify my spirit

Angel of Ether, please gather the quintessence

THE INVOCATION OF THE FIRST SEAL

*B*EINGS *of the Pure Light and the Holy Higher worlds,*
we stand here before you in communion and reverence.

We lift up our hearts and hold our minds pure for the duration
of this Invocation.

We seek to align ourselves with the highest harmonies
and frequencies of intelligence and light, that they may pierce us
to the core of our being, opening us to the arch of the infinite,
and coaxing us softly into the arms of our essence.

> *We come to invoke the first Divine Ray,*
> *that we may partake of its Grace.*

In our journey through the Seven Rays and their gifts of Grace,
there is a natural flow of Involution as the forces of Divine shakti
enter our bodies and beings. Here in the First Ray we come
to the deepest layers of the form. Here we find the oldest patterns,
the most stubborn karma, the tenderest wounds of all.

> *We tread softly as we approach such Holy ground.*
> *We mythically remove our shoes as we approach this*
> *precious inner place.*

The First Holy Ray was the first place in which our deepest
potential and realization was sealed at the mythical fall.
When working with the first Ray we come to the basis,
to the foundation, to the conception.

> *We come to the core.*

*We acknowledge that this is not a place to tread without
preparation. Each of the other 6 Rays prepare us for this place.
Each Ray leads to another, each Seal conceals another.
The mystery of their opening is beyond teachings, beyond words.
In every journey there is a final test, a drop into the void,
an encounter with Divine doubt, a final, thunderous cleansing.
This is the place that lies beyond the First Sacred Seal.*

> *We come before you naked.
> We give up everything.
> We draw the Holy Valour of the masters into our lungs.
> We close our eyes and we prepare ourselves
> for this great inner test.
> All that we have accomplished we leave behind,
> all our victories, our moments of great love, our ecstasies...
> We realise that we cannot carry anything beyond this point.*

*We bring before you our very identity.
We bring before you our wisdom, our love,
all our prayers and our Truth.
We bring before you our loved ones,
our children and all that we consider most essential and precious.*

> *We surrender all these worldly attachments into this First Seal.*

*We come to acknowledge that there is a force locked inside us —
a force of such power and intelligence, and this force is repressed.
It is choked by our fear.*

*We come here to face the depths of our fear.
Whenever we are willing to face our fear,
we are looking into this First Holy Seal.*

Beyond this Seal lies the void.

We prepare ourselves to be washed,
to be emptied, to be expunged.
We give ourselves up entirely to the darkness,
and we do so knowing that somewhere, somehow,
hidden in this darkness, we will rediscover the light.

We invoke the frequency of Incandescence,
The Holy inner Light of this primary Ray.

We have travelled for so long through the wilderness, through the
wasteland, through the endless winters of consciousness.
We are tired, we are worn to the bone. There is nothing left in us.
All of a sudden in the darkness and the cold gloom, we see a tiny
light far off, a beacon of warmth, a flame of hope.

This is the tiny ember of incandescence.
It can never be extinguished.
No matter how great the surrounding darkness,
no matter how oppressive the weight of our pain,
this tiny spark remains.
We softly fan this spark.
We approach the light in the gloom.
It is a hearth-light, a family home.
We knock on the door. It opens.
A friendly face greets us and welcomes us in, weary traveller.

We are given a seat by the open fire. We take off our icy
boots, we wash our aching feet in warm fresh water,
and we breathe a sigh of relief as the waves of exhaustion and
loss are magically washed away.

We have found home.
It is deep within our bellies, this ember.
Its warm gold glow is always present.
Whenever we are overwhelmed, whenever we are afraid,
we can find it in the dark.
We learn now to fan the ember,
to place the tinder of our love around it,
to gently, ever so softly blow on the spark.
And so it grows. And so it grows. And as it grows,
so our hearts are rekindled.
Hope dawns, faith returns.
Love pours back through our bodies.
So many incarnations, so many lives, so much effort,
so much suffering, so much pain, so much fear.
And we let it all go, and the light is there.

How can this be?
What is this Grace that has placed this tenderest essence
within us?
How could we have forgotten?
How can we have missed this essential truth,
this delicate Truth?
We embrace the simplicity of our own incandescence.
We warm ourselves with this flame — this sacred flame
of Shambala — the hidden light within the form.
We build the blaze, carefully placing the logs here and there —
not too many at first.
With great care we build this immortal pyre.

We attune ourselves to the light of the star Arcturus.

Great Guardian, Keeper of the Bear, Beneficent One,
Uplifted One, Star of Wheat, Star of Joy. Aeons you have
guarded our galaxy, watched over our growth and our lives.
Even as we plunged from the heavenly realms down into
the lost worlds of the form, long have you waited
and witnessed our forgetting.
Your orange gold glow has been our ember of hope.
You remind us of home,
of the place where the sun rises, of the world before the wound.
Let us draw your soft trusting glow into our hearts,
into our bellies, into the soles of our tired feet.
Let us sigh now as we sit at your hearth,
your warm-blooded hearth.

We use your light, your gift to build our inner fire,
our cosmic fire.
We nurture this precious fire.
We let it grow and glow.
We draw in your warmth
We feel awe as your power grows inside us,
filling us with strength, pouring through us,
expanding now through our chest,
through our organs and our skin.
We revel in your welcoming long-lost embrace.

We bring special attention now to the first layer of all our
subtle bodies, our physical form and its etheric counterpart.

Here in this densest matter, we feel your burning compassion.
We feel the healing warmth of all the layers of the 7 Rays hidden
behind incandescence. As we fan the flames of this light, of this
vast reservoir of love, so the pathways and meridians open up,

so the organs relax, so the cells come into synergy, into harmony.
One by one, our cells begin to burn. They begin to be transmuted.
They begin to ascend. As we draw down the layers of lights
deeper and deeper into this form, so in time we begin
to lighten up. Old illnesses, old ailments, old pains feel the flood
of your incandescent warmth.
We are self-healing. Life is self-healing.

We acknowledge the perseverance and commitment
it takes to vibrate the inner light of these physical cells.

We are now alive in the stream of the First Ray.
We give thanks for this special Gift of Divine Will.

Your Will, the clear will of the whole,
will be done on earth as it is in heaven.
Our souls soar on the memory of this future now.
We are here in this form, captured in the illusion of time,
but in truth we are free from time
for the Truth of your presence is always here now.
We implore your great will, your great hand, to work in our lives,
to work through us, to take command of our personality,
to reforge us anew in your white hot fire.

We surrender to Divine Will.
We surrender our weakness, our hopelessness.
Not my will, but thy Will be done.

We prepare to receive the great Archangel Mikhael.

Mikhael, angel of our Age, wielder of the sword of light.
We recognize your cry of 'Who is like God?'

You great protector of the Godhead.
None may pass through your Holy Seal without being completely
purified of all vanity. Thus you wield your sword of truth to grub
out the roots of ancestral karma,
of identification with the world of form.
We ask that you cut our attachments, that you open our hearts
as widely as your own. We ask to bask in the fires
of your knowing,
the fires of your valour, the fires of your faith.
We acknowledge your presence within us.
We bow to receive the cuts of your Grace,
as your smouldering sword of truth, alive with the blue flames of
the Will of God, shears off our hurts, our afflictions, our wound.
We trust so much in your deep love, as you prune us of our
vanity with your battle-cry of 'Who is like God?'

We humbly request the opening of the First Seal.

We know that once this seal has opened,
the floodgates are open.
We agree to accelerate our karma.
We agree to a parley with the dragon,
the ancient force of transmutation.
We allow our bodies to become the battlefield of the Gods,
with the great Mikhael at their head,
swinging his Divine sword in an arc of love,
cleansing and purifying, transforming and igniting,
singing with the harmony of all the Buddhas,
all the Divine hierarchies, as far as the Godhead itself.

We ask Mikhael for courage to surrender to these forces within us
so far beyond our ken.

We surrender our fear. Ancient memory lodged in the cells.
Tremor of Truth locked in the form.
We stand firm and anchored in our courage, knowing that fear
need not be feared, merely passed through with loving kindness.
We acknowledge the fear rooted in the form of all un-liberated beings.
We resonate with them, we empathize with the challenges
faced by all.
We forgive them their blindness, their foolishness, their ignorance,
their indifference. We forgive ourselves in the same breath.
All is clear. All is open.
The Seals remain always open for our healing.
We have only to ask for their Grace.
We have only to be present with our deepest longings and fears.

We rejoice above all, at the coming of Divine Will.
We feel it in our bodies as a tremor of Truth.
We sense its descent into all forms within
the mystery and illusion of time.
We anticipate our own freedom,
at whatever level it has awakened within us.
We trust in its furtherance.
We tremble in our atoms with the awe of your coming,
of the coming of the kingdom of heaven on earth.
We sense its silence.
We remember its completion,
and we rejoice in the perfection of its unravelling.

We feel the deep relaxation at our core as your Will enters our DNA,
the final vestige of our separateness.
We yield to the Will of the Whole.
We anticipate the supernova as your Will organizes our lower
trinity of subtle bodies to allow the full transmission of the trinity
of the higher subtle bodies.

We allow you to reorganize our lower life — our diet,
our movement, our feelings, our words, our thoughts
and our daily decisions.
We yield all up to you.
We yield to the Will of the Whole.
We become the great Seal, the Seal of Solomon, an integrated
field of Divine presence. The perfect balance of Truth,
Wisdom and Love.
We rest in the great mystery of the Six Rays, the six bodies
and their culmination and envelopment in the mystical Seventh.

We give great thanks for this secret teaching
of these Seven Sacred Seals.
We digest its transmission at the level that is most natural for us.
We also allow it to stretch our awareness, to quicken our
evolution and to bring our hearts and minds into the highest
resonance with the great beings who guard each Seal.
We open to receive the myriad colours and frequencies
of radiance and light.
We give ourselves the generosity of time
to let these truths percolate inside our physicality.
We give over our bodies entirely to your Grace.

We bring this Invocation to a close
with the Blessing of the Five Elements.

Amen.

THE SEVEN SACRED SEALS

PART 5

PRAYERS, INVOCATIONS & FORMULAS
TO ACCOMPANY THE SEVEN SEALS

THE PRAYER OF TRANSMUTATION

(Holding palm on belly)

A NGELS and Beings of the Pure Light,
please help me to purify and transmute this dense,
low frequency karmic energy into love, into light, into purity,
into Truth, into the spirit of Divine Tenderness.

INVOCATION OF THE ILLUMINATI
For Synarchy and Harmony

*B*EINGS *of the higher worlds,*
I salute you. I seek to align myself
with the highest harmony of the heavenly realms.
I make all seven layers of my being available
as a harp for your blessed fingers.
Please attune and bring into harmony
the multicoloured strings of my Self.

(Pause)

In deep harmony with the Ideal of Heaven on Earth,
I align myself with the Great White Brotherhood
I align myself with the Great Sapphire Sisterhood
I align myself with the Planetary and Celestial Synarchy
May my vehicle be used as a blueprint
for the incarnation of this great Ideal
May the beings from higher evolutions work through me,
bringing Grace and harmony to all that I do.

BLESSING OF THE ANGELS OF THE FIVE ELEMENTS

A NGEL *of Earth, please purify my physical body (3 breaths)*
Angel of Water, please purify my astral body (3 breaths)
Angel of Air, please purify my mental body (3 breaths)
Angel of Fire, please sanctify my spirit (3 breaths)
Angel of Ether, please gather the quintessence (3 breaths)

OPTIONAL MOVEMENTS

The arms lie open at your sides and gradually form a
great arc as you reach up to the sky. Your palms come
together above your head just as you summon the Angel
of Fire, and as you sanctify your spirit, your palms come
down to rest in prayer position over your heart. Finally,
as you summon the Angel of Ether, your hands come to
rest face down on your belly.

PRAYER FOR ILLNESS

I call upon the great being we know as Raphael,
Archangel of Healing and Love.
Raphael, friend of all humans and all sentient creatures,
please bring your deep red-gold healing light into my body.
Let your warmth flow through the many subtle layers
of my energy body.
May you stitch up the rent in the fabric of my being.
May your light lead my intuition to the place where healing
is most needed.
May your radiance imbue me with vigour.
May your love inspire me with a quiet knowing
of the perfection of this illness.
May I learn greater compassion
through the gift of this suffering.
May I dedicate more of my being to the service of the whole.
I dedicate this suffering to the service and healing of the whole.
I hold you close for as long as I need you.
I thank you for the Grace of this suffering.

PRAYER OF DEEP SERENITY

*D*IVINE *Mother, I come before you*
naked and vulnerable.
Please allow me to enter
your sacred womb-space.
Please help me to settle into
the infinite peace of your arms.
Please bring me the deep, gentle patience
of the pregnant mother.
Everything happens at the perfect time.
Everything is for the great Good.
Please suffuse me with your deep Serenity.
Please soften my heart and remind me
of my true home.

PRAYER OF MANIFESTATION
AND DIVINE SERVICE

*A*NGELS *and Beings of the higher worlds,*
please help me to bring this wish into form.
I ask this thing in order to align more deeply
with my higher purpose and so that I can be
of greater service to the whole.

Please help me manifest the very highest possible potential
within the limitations of this form. Purify my aura constantly
in order for higher forces to work through me. I make my body,
heart and soul available for your pure emanations. Make me
an instrument of your Wisdom, your Love and your Truth.

THE RAINBOW BLESSING OF THE ARCHANGELS

*M*IKHAEL *Angel of Divine Will,*
Bless my physical body with
the Ray of Incandescence

Khamael, Angel of Omniscience,
Bless my astral body with
the Ray of Phosphorescence

Raphael, Angel of Universal Love,
Bless my mental body with
the Ray of Rubescence

Haniel, Angel of Epiphany,
Bless my causal body with
the Ray of Iridescence

Tsadkiel, Angel of Forgiveness,
Bless my buddhic body with
the Ray of Pearlescence

Gabriel, Angel of Truth,
Bless my atmic body with
the Ray of Quiescence

Tsaphkiel, Angel of Grace,
Bless my monadic body with
the Ray of Luminescence

HOLY INCANTATION OF SOLACE

LET love flow through my soul
Let light flower in my heart
Let warmth radiate my belly
Let purity shimmer in my bones
Let kindness resound in my voice
Let clarity shine through my mind
Let solace abound in my life
Touching all who I meet
Let solace abound in the world
bringing all beings into perfect union.

PRAYER OF THANKS

THANK you my Lord, my face
For pouring into me
For ladling your love into my heart.

Thank you for each happening in my life
For offering me the chance
To pocket your Grace.

Thank you for waiting for me
when I forget who I am
and even when I forget you.

Thank you my Lord, my heart
For constantly cradling me
In your tender mother's arms

And for each day of my life
in this luminous world.
Thank you. Thank you. Thank you.

THE LADY'S PRAYER

*O*UR *Lady, who lives at the heart of all form,*
Hallowed be thy name.
May thy Queendom come,
May thy Will be done
That heaven may come to earth.

Please allow me this day
To drink from your sacred, silver spring
And forgive me my forgetting
As I learn through your Grace
To return all non love with Love,

And take me by the hand
And lead me step by step
Into the patient valley of your Heart

For yours is the earth, my body and my life
For ever and ever.

Amen

May Grace be with you

CPSIA information can be obtained
at www.ICGtesting.com
Printed in the USA
BVHW020311180419
545812BV00016B/288/P